Instructional Routines Handbook

Mc
Graw
Hill
Education

mheducation.com/prek-12

Send all inquiries to:
McGraw-Hill Education
Two Penn Plaza
New York, New York 10121

ISBN: 978-0-07-697907-3
MHID: 0-07-697907-5

Printed in the United States of America.

8 9 10 11 12 LWI 27 26 25 24 23   E

Table of Contents

Welcome to *Wonders*

Routines

Welcome to
WONDERS

Wonders is a comprehensive literacy solution designed to meet the challenges of today's classroom and reach all learners in Kindergarten through Grade 6.

A wealth of print and digital resources provide unmatched support for building strong literacy foundations, accessing complex texts, supporting English Language Learners, genre writing, writing to sources, and building social emotional skills. *Wonders* provides your students equity of access to rich texts and rigorous instruction and gives you the tools to meet the needs of all of your students.

What
WONDERS
Can Do...

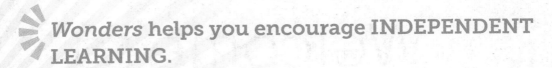 *Wonders* helps you encourage INDEPENDENT LEARNING.

Gradual Release of Responsibility The Gradual Release of Responsibility model provides you with an instructional framework for moving from teacher knowledge to student understanding and application. The Gradual Release of Responsibility framework, paired with *Wonders'* rigorous and challenging curriculum, ensures that all students are supported as they acquire the skills and strategies necessary for success. We provide you with the tools to

- explain and model your thinking;
- intentionally prompt, cue and question students;
- provide opportunities for collaboration;
- have students practice independently.

The Gradual Release of Responsibility model is not linear. Your students can move back and forth between each of the components as they master skills and strategies.

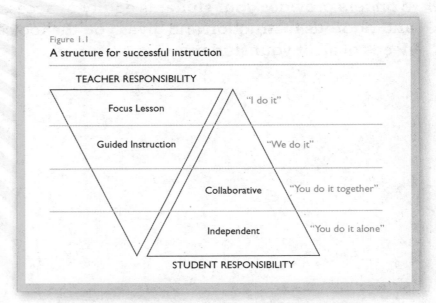

Figure 1.1
A structure for successful instruction

TEACHER RESPONSIBILITY

Focus Lesson — "I do it"

Guided Instruction — "We do it"

Collaborative — "You do it together"

Independent — "You do it alone"

STUDENT RESPONSIBILITY

According to *Wonders* author Dr. Douglas Fisher, "Gradual Release of Responsibility is transferring—slowly and intentionally—information, knowledge, skills and strategies to learners."

Here's how the Gradual Release of Responsibility works:

I Do This is where you explain and model to your students what it is they are learning to do.

We Do In this step, you and your students work together and share the instruction. Students get to practice while you guide and teach.

You Do, I Watch After students have had the chance to practice with you, it's time for them to practice on their own. This is where you observe and offer corrective feedback as students collaborate and practice.

You Do It Alone After modeling, showing, guiding, and allowing them to practice, it's time for your students to work independently.

Student-Driven Learning Student-driven learning is exactly what it sounds like. It is a classroom filled with students getting the instruction they need at the moment they need it. Your students are at the center of instruction. In a classroom where learning is student-driven, there are lots of small groups, collaborative conversations, digital tools that encourage literacy, and choices for self-selected and independent reading and writing available.

In *Wonders*, students are encouraged to express their ideas, apply what they are learning, self-monitor their own progress, and direct and monitor the discussions they have with their classmates. And this encourages critical thinkers and helps students engage, make connections, and develop the confidence to read and reflect on complex texts. This helps students become independent learners.

Differentiated Learning When you think of differentiated learning, the first thing that may come to mind is small group instruction. But differentiated learning is more than that. It is a flexible approach to teaching so that your instruction meet the needs of all students.

Look for the Differentiated Reading and Writing boxes in your **Teacher's Editions**. They provide guidance on how to use Whole Group lessons with Approaching Level, On Level, Beyond Level students, as well as English Language Learners. In addition to the scaffolded Differentiated Reading and Writing boxes, you will find lessons with support for English Language Learners, with Spotlight on Language Features woven throughout.

There are also Teach in Small Group Options boxes to help you teach flexibly by differentiating instruction for all students. Based on the needs of your students, you decide whether to teach the lesson in whole group or small group. The instruction in the boxes helps you tailor the lessons to the needs of your students.

Differentiate instruction and accelerate learning using your **Data Dashboard** and the Check for Success/Differentiate Small Group Instruction boxes at the end of each minilesson. You will also find just the right lesson at the end of each genre study to support your students in Approaching, On Level, or Beyond Small Groups. These lessons help your students build the skills they need.

> **❝ As you re-group students, think about their learning gaps as well as opportunities to validate and extend their thinking. Form groups focused on specific instructional and learning goals. And remember, some students need to be part of a few groups, and some students only need one group. ❞**
>
> **— Dr. Douglas Fisher**

Wonders helps you make LEARNING VISIBLE.

Learning Goals and Student Outcomes Learning goals and student outcomes help your students know what to expect. That's important because when teachers provide a clear purpose for what their students will learn, it encourages new learning and increases student understanding. *Wonders* author Dr. Douglas Fisher says that every day and in every lesson, students should know what they will be learning and what that learning will look like. He also says that students need to be told. They shouldn't have to infer what their teachers want them to learn.

Learning goals establish a purpose for learning and ensure that both students and teachers have the same idea as to what is going on in the classroom. Strong learning goals are specific, measurable, action-focused, relevant, and trackable. Student outcomes target the learning your students will do.

So what do learning goals and student outcomes look like? Here are some examples from the *Wonders* Grade 3 Unit 1 **Teacher's Edition.**

Objectives	Learning Goals What am I learning?	Why am I learning this?	Student Outcomes How will I know I have learned it?
Generate questions about text before, during, and after reading to deepen understanding and gain information.	Tell students that when they read, they may come across something they don't understand. They will learn to ask questions to clarify information. Then look for answers in the text.	**Think Aloud** As I read, I can pause to ask myself questions to check my understanding. Then I reread and paraphrase the text that answers my question.	I will be able to ask and answer questions to deepen understanding.
Explain how the author's use of text features supports understanding.	Explain to students that authors use text features, such as headings and maps, to help readers understand the events in the story and picture where they took place.	**Think Aloud** I see there are names of cities on the map. I can reread the text to see if it tells me where Kiku lived.	I will be able to use text features to better understand the text.

Genre: Fiction
- Has made up characters, and events
- Stories have a beginning, a middle, and an end
  May include dialogue
  - Dialogue is the words the characters say
  - Writers use quotation marks to show dialogue

Anchor Charts Another way you can make learning visible for your students is by creating anchor charts. According to *Wonders* author Kathy Bumgardner, when anchor charts are created with students, they are a valuable classroom resource to refer back to as they encounter other texts and learning scenarios.

Anchor charts are classroom resources created by you and your students. They provide visible cues to scaffold instruction and make instruction clear. The information on anchor charts supports lessons that you teach and then remind students of what they learned.

In *Wonders,* students in Grades K–6 help create and add to anchor charts that focus on the Essential Question, genre features, comprehension skills and strategies, vocabulary strategies, and writing. Anchor charts help students keep track of what they are learning.

Wonders author Kathy Bumgardner uses an anchor chart to help her students build knowledge.

Rubrics and Checklists Rubrics and checklists are great ways to assess your students' learning and make learning visible. A rubric is a tool that helps you evaluate the quality of your students' responses by listing skills and criteria for different levels of achievement. It also helps students see what is expected of them.

In *Wonders,* there are online rubrics and checklists. You can also create your own rubrics at **my.mheducation.com**.

In the **Reading/Writing Companion**, students can use a rubric, like the sample below, to figure out and score their own writing.

	Purpose, Focus & Organization (4pts)	Evidence & Details (4 pts)	Conventions (2 pts)	Total (10 pts)
My Score				

Track Your Progress Your students can self-assess and evaluate what they have learned using the *Wonders* Track Your Progress rubric at the end of each unit. On this page in the Reading/Writing Companion, your students have the chance to think about what they have learned and score how well they have met the learning objectives. In Grades 1–6, your students also have a chance to reflect in writing about something they want to improve and why. In Kindergarten, students have the same chance to reflect in a collaborative conversation with a partner.

Assessment Informs Instruction *Wonders* assessments allow you to monitor your students' progress through the curriculum in a steady and structured manner. You also can use them to better understand your students' performance by diagnosing their specific strengths and weaknesses. The accumulated data from the assessments, along with your personal observations, provide the information you need to inform subsequent instruction, aid in making leveling and grouping decisions, and point toward areas in need of reteaching or remediation.

Wonders helps you teach the WHOLE CHILD.

Habits of Learning Habits of Learning are a set of behaviors that support your students' learning and growth. In *Wonders*, we frame them as positive I-statements to empower learners.

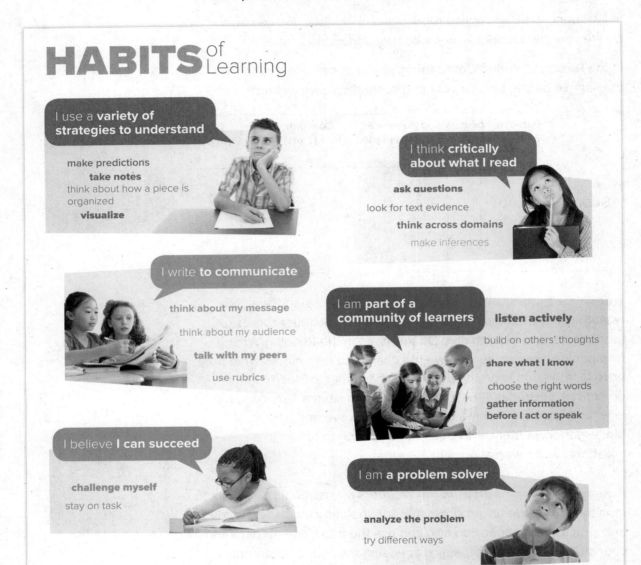

HABITS of Learning

I use a variety of strategies to understand

make predictions
take notes
think about how a piece is organized
visualize

I think critically about what I read

ask questions
look for text evidence
think across domains
make inferences

I write to communicate

think about my message
think about my audience
talk with my peers
use rubrics

I am part of a community of learners

listen actively
build on others' thoughts
share what I know
choose the right words
gather information before I act or speak

I believe I can succeed

challenge myself
stay on task

I am a problem solver

analyze the problem
try different ways

As you model, discuss, and nurture these habits all year long, students learn to see themselves as active, critical thinkers who read, write, and think with purpose. The habits will serve them well beyond your classroom, giving them the confidence and skills they need to thrive in school and in the workplace.

Each unit focuses on one habit of learning and provides opportunities to share and discuss how students are using them. Look for the Habits of Learning boxes in your **Teacher's Editions** for ideas and suggestions for building these habits.

Social Emotional Learning Social Emotional Learning helps students recognize emotions and develop social skills so they can express themselves effectively and work together productively. *Wonders* focuses on developing students' awareness and skills in these areas:

Social Emotional Learning

- Curiosity
- Creativity
- Logic and Reasoning
- Initiative
- Relationships and Pro-Social Behavior
- Social Problem-Solving
- Care and Empathy

- Feelings and Emotions
- Identity
- Belonging
- Self-Confidence
- Task Persistence
- Flexible Thinking
- Planning and Problem-Solving

In Kindergarten through Grade 5, *Wonders* integrates key social emotional learning competencies that will support learning and growth. These include working memory, focused attention, prosocial behaviors, task persistence, and many more.

In Kindergarten and Grade 1, social emotional lessons developed by Sesame Workshop includes engaging video assets focused on specific skills. These assets are supported by teacher lessons and home activities.

The development of social emotional learning continues throughout Grades 2–5. Each genre study explores a social emotional learning topic that relates to the study's Essential Question. As you discuss the texts in the genre study and engage in activities, help students understand the role the emotions and social skills play in stories and in life, and offer opportunities for them to develop and practice their own skills and strategies.

Classroom Culture Your classroom culture sets the tone for student interactions and learning. It supports the Habits of Learning and encourages the development of Social Emotional skills. *Wonders* helps you foster a positive classroom culture based on these guiding principles:

- We respect and value each other's experience.
- We learn through modeling and practice.
- We promote ownership of learning.
- We foster a love of reading.
- We inspire confident writers.
- We build knowledge.

Introduce these ideas as you build a sense of community during the first few weeks of school. Then revisit them throughout the year as you strengthen students' commitment to their community and to learning. To support this work, each unit focuses on one principle and provides opportunities to reflect on others.

Wonders helps you teach it YOUR WAY.

Wonders respects your expertise and recognizes that every teacher has a unique set of skills and personal teaching style that reaches students in a way that no one else can. We appreciate that you know your students better than almost anyone—their strengths, their needs, their interests—and that you do everything you can to make learning an empowering experience.

To support your work in the classroom, *Wonders* is designed to help you

- integrate your favorite resources or use our resources with your preferred approach or framework—including workshop-focused, blended learning, project-based learning, and authentic literature focused;

- provide student-centered learning, small-group teaching, and minilessons with embedded support for English Language Learners, gifted and talented students, and students in need of Tier 2 support;

- offer resources and tools that meet students where they are and take them where they need to be, in both print and digital formats;

- base instruction on research—and integrate best practices into the daily routine of your classroom;

- choose your pathway. Every time your class is ready to start a new text set, you may choose to explore authentic literature, focus on leveled readers and differentiated genre passages, or integrate independent reading with books that connect core concepts in each genre.

Reading Workshop If you use a reading workshop approach in your classroom, *Wonders* provides the resources and tools you need to support your instruction.

Text Resources Draw on these texts for read-alouds, whole-class mini-lessons, small-group strategy, guided reading lessons, or independent reading.

- **Interactive Read-Aloud Cards** The Interactive Read Aloud introduces the genre and reading strategy. Display these cards as you model the target reading strategy with the read aloud text.

- **Shared Reads** The short texts in the **Reading/Writing Companion** offer a chance to introduce the target skills and strategies of each genre study.

- **Literature Anthology** You'll find a rich collection of authentic literature and engaging informational texts in the main, paired, and independent reading selections. Each unit has a theme, and each genre study or week is organized around an Essential Question.
- **Leveled Readers** Each genre study or week has Leveled Readers for students who are Approaching, On Level, and Beyond grade level, as well as English Language Learners.
- **Differentiated Genre Passages** Designed to enrich and build knowledge, as well as provide more practice for skills and strategies, these short passages are at your students' levels. You can find lessons for these passages in the small group pages in your **Teacher's Editions.**
- **Classroom Library Books** Each one of these authentic and engaging trade books come with an online lesson plan with four pages of interactive student materials.

Minilesson Resources Draw on these resources as you plan your whole-class and small-group minilessons:

- **Shared Read prompts** highlight skills and strategies students should apply as they read.
- **Minilessons** follow each Shared Read and cover vocabulary strategies, reading strategies, genre characteristics, and literary elements or text features.
- **Craft and Structure lessons** develop inferential thinking skills and focus on author's craft.
- **Anchor text prompts** highlight skills and strategies students should apply as they read.

You'll find that *Wonders* is flexible. It gives options for teaching the Shared Read and Anchor Text in a whole class or a small group setting, based on the needs of your students. The Differentiated Reading boxes on the opening page of each of these sections provides guidance for how to use the lessons with small groups.

Small Group Lessons and Guided Reading Resources The Leveled Readers and Online Differentiated Genre Passages for each genre study can be used for strategy groups or guided reading groups. You may also use the Classroom Library selections and online lessons for your small groups. For additional texts, you can search the Leveled

Reader Database at **my.mheducation.com** by theme, keyword, genre, skill, text feature, grade range, Lexile, and Guided Reading level.

Independent Work In addition to reading independently from texts listed above or those of their own choice, students have options for independent work time, including

- responding to reading in their writer's notebooks;
- completing Workstation Activity Cards;
- reading with a partner;
- participating in literature circles or peer reading conferences;
- preparing a book talk.

See the Independent Reading section on pages 109–128 for additional strategies and more ideas.

Note that the Workstation Cards make it easy for you to provide literacy activities to engage the students who are not working with you in a small group. These cards enable you to create various stations where small groups of students can work independently on reading, writing, word study or content area activities.

Writing Workshop If you use a writing workshop approach in your classroom, *Wonders* provides a variety of options and tools you can draw from.

Writing Opportunities Students have varied opportunities to write throughout each genre study or week, including

- Respond to Reading prompts
- Research and Inquiry Projects
- Genre Writing
- Write to Multiple Sources

You can choose from these options based on your students' needs. Students can write in the **Reading/Writing Companion**, in their writer's notebook, or in an online writer's notebook.

Genre Writing Students learn to analyze an expert model and examine genre characteristics and author's craft techniques to transfer to their own writing. As you guide your students through the writing process you will also find mini-lessons to support them as they plan, draft, and revise their work.

Wonders provides rubrics that link to the skills taught during the genre study and encourages students to work with peers throughout the process. Students use these rubrics to self-assess their writing.

You'll also find suggestions for differentiating the writing instruction at the beginning of each instructional sequence. You can also draw on a variety of digital tools to support your instruction, including

- graphic organizers
- student models—draft, revised, and edited
- checklists for editing and peer conferencing
- videos for skills such as taking notes and evaluating sources

The grammar lessons in the **Teacher's Edition** can also be used as Writing Workshop mini-lessons, or you can use them with small groups of students as needed.

Writing to Multiple Sources Students learn how to respond to a writing prompt by reading a student model and sources. Then they analyze sources, take notes, and use a graphic organizer to craft an informed response. In these weeks, there are mini-lessons to support instruction, rubrics for self-assessment, and peer conferencing opportunities.

Digital Learning While a book, paper, and pencil are essential tools for students to grow as readers and writers, there are digital tools that can enhance and support student learning as well. Program core texts, such as the Shared Read, authentic Anchor Texts, Paired Texts, and Leveled Readers, are all provided in a multi-sensory eBook format that includes audio to support struggling readers and mark-up tools to support students in interacting with the text. When students login to *Wonders* they can easily access all the 'reads' aligned to that week—per the week on the teacher's calendar. Students can also launch an interactive display of the key vocabulary words of the week, which include audio/visual representations of the words. Another interactive component that is aligned to the skills of the week and easily accessed by students are the 'games'—practice activities that can then provide teachers with a printable report showing how students answered each question, thus informing a targeted and differentiated instructional path.

Putting It All Together

Wonders offers all the resources you need to plan and teach all year long. To help you put them together in the most effective way for you and your students, *Wonders* provides tools and professional development materials that can support you every step of the way.

Getting Started:

Start Smart In K–1, the first three weeks of instruction provide an introduction to the key instructional procedures that you will use throughout the year. We've designed this point-of-use professional development to get you up and running as efficiently as possible.

In Grades 2 and up, Start Smart is an overview of the instructional flow of each unit, highlighting the routines, lesson types, and resources that form the foundation of instruction.

my.mheducation.com Go online for a host of tools and resources to help you teach with *Wonders*, including

Teacher Dashboard You'll have easy access to weekly and daily lessons and the ability to customize lessons and resources based on your teaching style and students' needs. This tool also simplifies the process of printing or assigning student work, practice activities, and instructional games.

Data Dashboard This tool allows you to view student data in interactive tables and charts, making it easy to track students' work, identify students who have mastered a skill and those who need additional support, form groups, and chart student progress.

Professional Development Resources Here you'll find multimedia resources to get you up and running quickly and to dive deep into the research foundation of *Wonders*:

- Learn to Use Wonders
- Author White Papers
- Wonders Research Base
- Assessment
- Classroom Videos
- Coach Videos
- Digital Help
- WonderWorks
- English Learners

In the next section of the book, you'll find the instructional routines that provide the structure for much of the teaching in *Wonders*. Instructional Routines are a set of activities taught explicitly to students. They reflect best classroom practices and help your students focus on what they are learning, rather than learning a new way to do something. Once students are familiar with a routine, it can be used to teach new skills and content efficiently. In *Wonders*, instructional routines are comprised of carefully sequenced steps that follow the Gradual Release of Responsibility model.

The consistent structure of instructional routines allows students to focus on learning content because they know what to expect and what to do. Investing time in the beginning of the year teaching essential routines pays dividends throughout the year as students spend more time engaging in learning tasks and teachers have more opportunities to provide immediate feedback and differentiate instruction.

ROUTINES

In *Wonders,* the routines follow the same sequence of steps every time and slowly transfer the responsibility of the task to the students.

Routines

- effectively organize instruction;
- help set clear expectations for students;
- help teachers scaffold instruction;
- minimize instructional time and teacher talk ;
- maximize student participation.

Many of the instructional routines are included in the online Model Lessons Video Library.

In addition to instructional routines, look for a variety of activities and strategies at the end of each section. Many of these hands-on activities encourage multisensory learning which is one more way to help you meet the needs of all of your students.

Multisensory learning is instruction that teaches to more than one sense at a time. Engaging multiple senses can help students to acquire a stronger understanding of new skills and processes. You will find that these activities will benefit all of your students.

"Sharing ideas and working collaboratively are learned skills. Students benefit from instruction and practice that develops learning habits for listening attentively, sharing talking time, and communicating respectfully."

— Dr. Vicki Gibson

Sergiy Bykhunenko/iStockphoto/Getty Images

Collaborative
CONVERSATIONS

What You Need to Know About Collaborative Conversations

Collaborative conversations are rich, structured conversations around grade-level topics and texts. According to *Wonders* program author Dr. Douglas Fisher, they provide an important link between reading and writing by helping students clarify their thinking and learn to use academic language. Making collaborative conversations integral to your classroom culture not only gives your students opportunities to take ownership of their learning, but it also helps them to build knowledge. When students talk to each other they also learn how to listen and communicate with respect. Collaborative conversations give students the chance to develop their social emotional skills, such as social problem-solving, task persistence, and flexible learning.

To have effective collaborative conversations, students need to understand the expectations of the discussion and be held accountable for their participation. As their teacher, you need to explicitly teach your students how to interact during a collaborative conversation and how to document their learning. The Collaborative Conversation Routine helps you do that. You will find suggestions for both teaching expectations and fostering accountability in the Additional Strategies for Teaching Collaborative Conversations section on page 22.

Research

- Discussion-based practices improve student's thinking skills and comprehension of a text (Murphy, Wilkinson, Soter, Hennessey, & Alexander, 2009).

- In effective schools, classroom conversations about how, why, and what students read are important parts of the literacy curriculum (Applebee, 1996: Schoenbach, Greenleaf, Cziko & Hurwitz, 1999).

How Does *Wonders* Teach Collaborative Conversations?

Wonders provides many opportunities for students to engage in collaborative conversations, including

- at the beginning of every week or genre study, as you introduce the concept and talk about the Essential Question;
- every time you work through the Close Reading Routine;
- during guided practice and independent practice;
- when students respond to texts they are reading;
- when students write about text.

 **COLLABORATE** When you will see this logo in the **Teacher's Edition,** it indicates when a collaborative conversation is recommended. You'll find instructional support on each Talk About It page at the start of each genre study or week, and on the Peer Conferencing pages.

What Does Success Look Like?

As you observe students having collaborative conversations, be sure that they

- understand the focus of the conversation;
- are able to make statements and ask questions related to the focus;
- listen respectfully to one another;
- are capable of engaging in multiple exchanges that build on the ideas of others to clarify thinking and express new thoughts.

"That's a good inference. It helped me make a connection to one of the stories we read last week."

"I hadn't thought of it that way. Can you show me what part of the story made you think that?"

Routines

The Collaborative Conversation routine aligns with the lessons provided in the **Teacher's Edition**, but allows you to take a flexible approach so you can meet the needs of all your students.

Collaborative Conversation Routine

1. **Introduce the focus of the conversation.** Give students the topic they will discuss.

   In our discussion today, we'll be talking about how we can show that we are good citizens.

2. **Review relevant guidelines to support student participation.** Call attention to any guidelines or resources you want students to focus on. See the Collaborative Conversation mini posters on pages 25–27.

   As you talk, remember to wait for the other person to finish before you begin speaking.

3. **Provide specific information so students know exactly what to do.** Tell students how much time they have to discuss, who they are talking with (partner, small group, whole group), and what you expect them to do as a result of the conversation (e.g., take notes, write a reflection, share with the larger group).

   You will be talking with a partner for one minute. At the end of the conversation, you'll have a chance to share your ideas with the rest of the class.

4. **Monitor student conversations and provide corrective feedback as necessary.** Listen as students discuss to be sure they stay on topic and follow guidelines.

5. **Close the conversation(s).** Highlight positive behaviors and contributions.

   I noticed that all of you took turns and listened carefully to your partner. You also stayed on topic. And you had such good ideas to share with the rest of the class!

Corrective Feedback

Point out what students are doing right. Redirect discussions that may have gotten off track by suggesting statements or questions that will refocus the discussion. Encourage students to build on one another's exchanges.

Additional Strategies for Teaching Collaborative Conversations

Role Play a Collaborative Conversation. Invite a small group to model a collaborative conversation with you in front of the class, following each step of the routine. Pause throughout the conversation to point out examples of appropriate listening and sharing.

Display Sentence Starters and Frames. Scaffold effective collaborative conversations by discussing and posting sentence starters and frames to help students share their ideas, respond to others, disagree respectfully, clarify ideas, make connections, and ask questions. Encourage students to refer to the sentence starters and frames and to add to them when they find a new one.

> ## Sentence Starters
>
> I'm wondering...
>
> I figured out...
>
> I'm not sure I understand...
>
> Can you point to text evidence that shows...?
>
> I agree with you, but wonder about...
>
> Can you explain...?
>
> I'm confused. Please tell me more about...
>
> _____

Post a Word Bank. To boost students' understanding and use of academic language, create and post a word bank. Encourage them to refer to the word bank during their collaborative conversations.

Have Students Self-Evaluate. Regularly invite students to reflect on their conversations. Offer prompts such as the following: *What worked well in your conversations this week? What would you like to see happen differently next time? What's hard for you in a collaborative conversation? What was your favorite conversation this week? Why?* Have students evaluate their participation and set goals for future discussions.

Encourage Peer Feedback Periodically, ask pairs of students to observe conversations taking place in a whole-class setting. Give them a copy of your guidelines and ask them to note which rules are being observed and any helpful questions or statements students make that help to build knowledge or clarify thinking. After the conversation, review students' observations and discuss them with the whole group. As a class, set goals for future collaborative conversations.

Use the Collaborative Conversations Videos.

Use the "How to Have a Collaborative Conversation" checklists on pages 25–27. Then share the Collaborative Conversations Video: Small Goup Discussion with students. Use the lessons below as you replay and talk about the video.

Kindergarten and Grade 1

Share the Collaborative Conversations video with students. After the video, ask them to tell you what they noticed. *What did you notice about how the children in the video talked with each other?* Write their responses on chart paper.

Part 1: Initial group discussion (stop at 0:24) After watching the first part of the video, students should notice that the children in the video are not talking about the selection. *What are the children talking about?* (pigs and mud) *How do you know they are not staying on topic?* (They are sharing their opinions.)

Part 2: Teacher and group discussion (stop at 1:50) Discuss how the teacher helps the group review the rules. *How is the teacher helping the children?* (She reminds them of the rules for collaborative conversations. Then she reviews the discussion question and helps them think of key details.)

Part 3: Group discussion As students watch the end of the video again, help them note items on the checklist the children in the video are doing. *Do you notice anything the children can be doing that they are not? What might the children do better?* (They could have talked more about each other's comments. They could have talked more about the story, instead of their feelings.)

Grades 2 and 3

Share the Collaborative Conversations video with students. Ask them to take notes as they observe the group discussion. Then replay the video and stop at the following parts. Use the checklist on page 26 to discuss.

Part 1: Teacher and group discussion (stop at 1:12) Use the checklist to discuss how the teacher helps the group get ready for their collaborative conversation. (The teacher asks students to review the checklist. He gives them a discussion question.)

Part 2: Group discussion Have students work with a partner. Replay the last section of the video. *What items on the checklist do you see the students in the group doing?* Ask students to comment on what they observe and list things the group in the video could be doing better. (Students could ask more questions about other group members' comments.)

Grades 4–6

Share the Collaborative Conversations video with students. Ask them to take notes as they observe the group discussion. Then replay the video and stop at the following parts. Use the checklist on page 27 to discuss.

Part 1: Initial group discussion (stop at 0:19) Ask students what they noticed about the group discussion. (Lorenzo makes a comment without citing text evidence.)

Part 2: Teacher and group discussion (stop at 1:15) Discuss how the teacher helps the group discuss the rules and focus the collaborative conversation. *How is the teacher helping the students?* (The teacher gives the group a discussion question. She reviews the rules for a good group discussion.)

Part 3: Group discussion Have students work with a partner. Replay the last section of the video, and ask them to note items on the checklist they see the students in the group doing. Have students comment on what they observe and list things the group in the video could be doing better. (They went off topic a few times, but their discussion helped them reach a conclusion.)

How to Have a Collaborative Conversation

- ☐ Listen to the person speaking.

- ☐ Take turns speaking.

- ☐ Respect each other's feelings and ideas.

- ☐ Ask and answer questions about what others are saying about the text.

- ☐ Ask questions to get more information.

- ☐ Say your ideas clearly.

How to Have a Collaborative Conversation

- ☐ Listen to the person speaking.
- ☐ Ask questions if you don't understand something.
- ☐ Try to stay on topic.
- ☐ Take turns speaking.
- ☐ Respect each other's feelings and ideas.
- ☐ Come to the discussion prepared.
- ☐ Ask and answer questions about what others are saying about the text.
- ☐ Find text evidence to answer questions.
- ☐ Express your ideas clearly.

How to Have a Collaborative Conversation

- [ ] Listen respectfully to the person speaking and wait for your turn to talk.
- [ ] Ask questions about things you don't understand.
- [ ] Listen to and repeat directions.
- [ ] Be prepared to discuss and explore ideas about the text.
- [ ] Refer to the text to find meaning and cite text evidence.
- [ ] Ask and answer questions about what others are saying about the text.
- [ ] Listen carefully so that you can state in your own words the main points and reasons the speaker presents.
- [ ] Respect each other's feelings and ideas.
- [ ] Express your ideas clearly.

WORD Work

Build Foundational Skills

Word Work in *Wonders* refers to the explicit, systematic sequence of instruction provided for the foundational skills of phonological and phonemic awareness, phonics, structural analysis, high-frequency words, spelling, and vocabulary. *Wonders* offers daily Word Work lessons in K–2; in Grades 3 and beyond, there are weekly phonics lessons and daily spelling lessons.

Word Work is essential for all students because it helps them learn to decode and encode words they need while reading and writing. It also supports the rigorous vocabulary instruction *Wonders* offers, providing the tools students need to tackle new words they encounter in texts they read and hear.

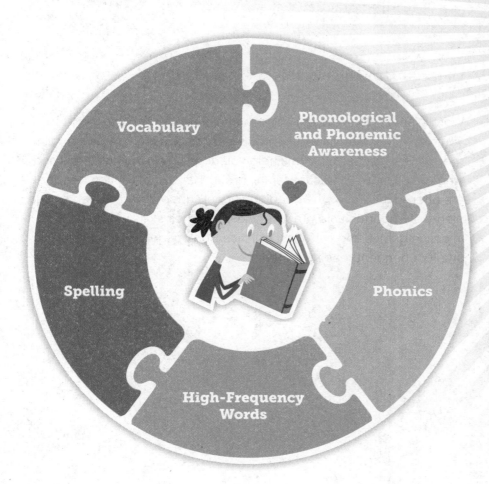

seamuss/Shutterstock

Integrated with Reading Instruction to Accelerate Growth

A strength of *Wonders* Word Work instruction is that it integrates phonological and phonemic awareness, phonics, and spelling skills with reading instruction to support and reinforce student learning. For example, in one week in Grade 2, the daily phonics lessons target long *u* spelled *u_e*, *ew*, *ue*, and *u*, which is also the focus of the daily spelling lessons and the phonemic awareness blending lesson. The Shared Read selection in the **Reading/Writing Companion** contains some long *u* words, as does the **Literature Anthology** selection for the genre study. The long-*u* spelling patterns are also featured in the week's decodable reader stories and in the Comprehension and Fluency passage on the corresponding page of the **Practice Book**.

> 66 All reading skills are only important to the extent that they help children comprehend what they are reading—and ultimately become highly motivated readers and writers. Be sure to link reading practice tasks to comprehension. 99
>
> —Dr. Jan Hasbrouck

Differentiated Instruction and Practice to Support All Students

Word Work lessons are quick, engaging, flexible, and differentiated. You can teach them as whole-group lessons or use them with small groups. Regular assessments help you determine who has a skill and who needs more instruction; small-group Tier 2 intervention lessons are offered for those who need additional support. And students have plenty of opportunity to practice and apply their skills independently, in online games and activities, Practice Book pages, leveled readers, and independent reading material.

Phonological and Phonemic Awareness

What You Need to Know About Phonological and Phonemic Awareness

Phonological awareness is the ability to hear, identify, and manipulate sounds in spoken words. It includes being able to detect rhymes, clap syllables, count words in sentences, and blend and segment onsets and rimes. Phonemic awareness is a subset of phonological awareness that refers specifically to the understanding that there are individual sounds, or phonemes, in words, such as the three phonemes /s/ /i/ /t/ in *sit* or /d/ /a/ /sh/ in *dash*. Phonemic awareness tasks include being able to isolate, identify, categorize, blend, segment, add, delete, substitute, and reverse individual phonemes.

Both phonological and phonemic awareness involve the auditory and oral manipulation of sounds, which are the prerequisite skills students need to understand print-based phonics instruction—and become successful readers.

> " Phonological awareness refers to the ability to perceive and manipulate the sounds within spoken language, independent of meaning. This awareness includes the ability to distinguish words, syllables, and phonemes and to recognize rhyme. Phonemic awareness is only one aspect of phonological awareness. "
> — Dr. Timothy Shanahan

Research

- Research indicates that the most critical phonemic awareness skills are blending and segmenting, since they are most closely associated with early reading and writing growth (NICHHD, 2001).

- Phonemic awareness has a positive overall effect on reading and spelling and leads to lasting reading improvement.

- Phonological processing problems are a significant factor in students experiencing reading difficulties, including dyslexia (International Dyslexia Association, 2017).

- Phonemic awareness instruction can be effectively carried out by teachers. It doesn't take a great deal of time to bring many children's phonemic awareness abilities up to a level at which phonics instruction begins to make sense.

How Does *Wonders* Teach Phonological and Phonemic Awareness?

The Word Work lessons in the *Wonders* K–2 **Teacher's Editions** include explicit, sequential, and systematic lessons. *Wonders* lessons teach sounds in sequence, moving from easier to more complex. Instruction begins with continuous sounds (e.g., /s/) before moving on to words that begin with stop sounds (e.g., /b/). Words that begin with one consonant are taught before words that begin with consonant blends or digraphs. All the phonological and phonemic awareness lessons follow a consistent, gradual release approach that also provides guidance for giving students corrective feedback. Instruction is fast-paced and differentiated, so students get the level of support and amount of practice they need to develop their skills. Phonemic awareness instruction occurs in Grades K–1 for all students and Grades 2 and beyond for students who need the support.

In addition to the Word Work lessons, *Wonders* provides a variety of resources to complement your instruction and student practice. You'll find additional practice for phonological and phonemic awareness skills in the weekly **Practice Book** page and online at **my.mheducation.com**. You'll find more support for instruction in the Tier 2 Intervention Phonemic Awareness Small Group Lessons.

What Does Success Look Like?

Observe students during the Guided Practice and Practice sections of the Word Work lessons. Students should be able to hear and understand that words are made up of sounds. They should be able to orally generate rhymes; clap syllables; and blend, segment, and manipulate the sounds in words.

McGraw-Hill Education

Routines

The routines in this section are integrated within the lessons provided in your **Teacher's Edition** but allow you to take a flexible approach to teaching phonological and phonemic awareness so you can meet the needs of all your students.

Phonological and Phonemic Awareness Routines

- Sentence Segmentation
- Identify and Generate Rhyme
- Syllable Segmentation
- Onset and Rhyme Blending
- Onset and Rime Segmentation
- Phoneme Categorization

- Phoneme Blending
- Phoneme Segmentation
- Phoneme Deletion
- Phoneme Substitution
- Phoneme Addition
- Phoneme Reversal

Sentence Segmentation Routine

This routine helps students distinguish the words within a sentence. It is used in the beginning of kindergarten as students develop phonological awareness.

1. **Explain** Explain to students that knowing how many words are in a sentence they hear is an important step in learning to read and write. Tell students that you will read a poem, nursery rhyme, or other short text. Then you will reread it to count the number of words they hear in each line.

2. **Model** Read aloud a short text all the way through. Then model how to count the words you hear in a line.

   Now I am going to reread the first line of our nursery rhyme. For each word I hear, I will hold up a finger. This will help me count the number of words in the line. [Say the first line, holding up a finger as you say each word:] Jack and Jill. *How many words did I say* (3)

3. **Guided Practice** Continue reading the short text line by line, asking student to hold up a finger for each word they hear.

   Now listen to the next line. Hold up one finger for each word, and we'll count the words.

4. **Practice** Students can practice independently by completing related pages from the **Practice Book** or doing Phonological Awareness Activities online.

Teaching Tip

You can also use sticky notes to represent and count sounds.

Corrective Feedback

If students hold up the wrong number of fingers, say the line again slowly and hold up a finger for each word. Then have students do it with you before proceeding to the next line.

Identify and Generate Rhyme Routine

Teaching Tip

Clearly state why words rhyme. Point out the part of the word that is the same (the rime, or vowel and consonant(s) that follow it). For example, say: *These words both end in /et/.*

Corrective Feedback

When students make mistakes identifying rhymes, say a rhyming pair of words and guide them to hear the rhyme. Say: *Let's check to see if* set *and* met *rhyme. Listen:* set, /s/ /et/; set *ends in /et/;* met, /m/ /et/, met *ends in /et/. Do* set *and* met *both end in /et/? Yes.*

When students make mistakes generating rhymes, segment the part of the word that must rhyme (e.g., */et/ in* set). Guide students to add consonants, consonant blends, and consonant digraph sounds to the beginning of the rime (e.g., /b/ /et/, /st/ /op/) to form rhyming words.

1. **Explain** Briefly explain the routine and its purpose.

   Today we will be listening for words that rhyme. Rhyming words have the same ending sounds. We will then make a list of rhyming words.

2. **Model** Model for students how to identify and then generate rhyming words.

   I am going to say two words. Listen: let, met. *Do* let *and* met *rhyme? Yes, they rhyme because they both end in the sounds /et/. Listen /l/ /et/,* let; /m// /et/, met.

   What other words rhyme with let *and* met? *I'll think of words that end in /et/. The word* set *ends in /et/, so* set *rhymes with* let *and* met.

3. **Guided Practice** Have children identify rhyming words using multiple word sets. Do the first set with students.

   Now let's try it together. I will say two words. If the words rhyme, stand up.

let, lot	bet, pet
let, beg	tell, sell

   Let's try some harder ones. I will say three words. Tell me which two words in the group rhyme.

led, bad, red	man, met, set
let, beg, get	sent, sand, bent

   Now let's see how many rhyming words we can say for each of the following words: red, let, beg, well, hen.

4. **Practice.** Students can practice independently by completing related pages from the **Practice Book** or doing Phonological Awareness Activities online. See Additional Strategies and Tips for Teaching Phonological Awareness on page 45 for more ideas for independent practice.

Syllable Segmentation Routine

1. **Explain** Briefly explain the routine and its purpose.

   We will listen for the number of beats we hear in a word. Each beat will have one vowel sound. We will clap each time we hear a beat. We call these beats syllables.

2. **Model** Demonstrate how to segment three or four words by syllable.

   Listen: basket. Now I will clap the beats, or syllables: bas (clap) ket (clap). Basket *has two syllables.*

3. **Guided Practice** Have students practice segmenting words by syllable.

   Clap these words with me. The number of claps is the number of syllables in the word.

basket (2)	Monday (2)	silly (2)	tomorrow (3)
yesterday (3)	desk (1)	chalkboard (2)	rhinoceros (4)
potato (3)	California (4)	cafeteria (5)	tumble (2)

4. **Practice** Students can practice independently by completing related pages from the **Practice Book** or doing Phonological Awareness Activities online. See Additional Strategies and Tips for Teaching Phonological Awareness on page 45 for more ideas for independent practice.

Teaching Tip

If students have difficulty clapping syllables, have them place their hands underneath their chin. Tell them that as they say a word, a new syllable happens every time their chin drops.

Onset and Rime Blending Routine

In this routine, students learn to blend an onset and rime to say a word. The rime is the vowel and everything after it in a syllable. The onset is everything before the rime. The onset can be a consonant, a consonant blend, or a digraph. Initially, teach this routine with onsets that are continuous single sounds (e.g., /f/, /l/, /r/, /s/, /v/, and /z/). Then, blend words with onsets that are stop sounds (e.g., /b/, /d/, /g/), and lastly, proceed to onsets that are consonant blends and digraphs.

1. **Explain** Briefly explain the routine and its purpose.

   Today, we will be blending, or putting together, the first sound(s) and the end part of a word to make a whole word.

2. **Model** Provide several models of how to blend the first sound(s) (onset) and the end part (rime) of a word.

   I will put sounds together to make a word. I'll say the first sound and then the end of the word. Then I will blend them together to say the word. Listen: /s / /at/. What is the word? The word is sat.

3. **Guided Practice** Have students practice blending words by onset and rime. Do the first word with them. Then, blend as a group.

   Listen to the word parts. Blend, or put together, the word parts to say the whole word.

/s/ /ad/	/m/ /at/	/f/ /ish/
/l/ /ip/	/r/ /un/	/n/ /est/

   Now let's try some harder ones. Listen to the word parts. Blend, or put together, the word parts to say the whole word.

/h/ /ad/	/b/ /at/	/c/ /ab/
/sl/ /ip/	/sp/ /un/	/ch/ /est/

4. **Practice** Have students blend words on their own.

   Listen to the word parts. Blend them together to say the whole word.

/v/ /an/	/r/ /ap/	/n/ /od/
/d/ /og/	/sh/ /ip/	/dr/ /op/

For more independent practice, students can complete related pages from the **Practice Book** or do Phonological Awareness Activities online. See Additional Strategies and Tips for Teaching Phonological Awareness on page 45 for more ideas.

Corrective Feedback

If students have difficulty blending onsets and rimes, repeat the routine with the same word, and then ask students to blend the word without you. Go back and repeat the last two examples before proceeding with a new example. Some students who struggle may need to go back to the easier task of blending syllable by syllable (e.g., napkin, /nap/ /kin/).

Onset and Rime Segmentation Routine

For students that have difficulty with Phoneme Segmentation, scaffold instruction by having them segment each word into its onset and rime.

1. **Explain** Briefly explain the routine and its purpose.

   We will be taking apart the sounds in a word we hear. We will say the first sound and then the rest of the word.

2. **Model** Provide several models of how to segment an onset and rime.

   I will take apart a word: sat. The first sound in sat is /s/. The end part of sat is /at/. Listen: sat, /s/ /at/.

3. **Guided Practice** Have students practice segmenting words by onset and rime. Do the first word with students.

   Listen to the word parts. Take apart the word. Say the first sound, then say the rest of the word.

sad /s/ /ad/	**mat** /m/ /at/
fun /f/ /un/	**lip** /l/ /ip/

   Now let's try some harder ones.

wish /w/ /ish/	**ship** /sh/ /ip/
thin /th/ /in/	**chest** /ch/ /est/

4. **Practice** Students can practice independently by completing related pages from the **Practice Book** or doing Phonological Awareness Activities online. See Additional Strategies and Tips for Teaching Phonological Awareness on page 45 for more ideas for independent practice.

Corrective Feedback

When students make mistakes during segmenting, model how to segment the onset and rime. Repeat the routine using the same word, asking students to respond without you. Go back and repeat the last two examples before proceeding with additional examples. Some students who struggle segmenting onset and rime will need to go back to the easier segmentation task of segmenting syllable by syllable (e.g., basket, /bas/ /ket/).

Phoneme Categorization Routine

Use the following instructional sequence to help students identify and categorize sounds at the beginning, at the end, or in the middle of words in a set.

1. **Explain** Briefly explain the routine and its purpose.

   Today we will be listening for words that have something in common. We will listen for words that begin with the same sound.

2. **Model** Model by saying three words, two of which begin with the same sound.

   I will say three words. Listen carefully to the beginning sound in each word. Tell me which word does NOT belong. Set, sad, man. (Stretch the initial sound in each word as you say it.) *Which word doesn't belong? That's right.* Man *begins with a different sound. Listen: /ssset/.* Set *begins with /s/. /sssad/.* Sad *begins with /s/. /mmman/.* Man *begins with /m/.*

Corrective Feedback

When students make a mistake with a word that begins with a continuous sound (/f/, /l/, /m/, /n/, /r/, /s/, /v/, /w/, /y/, or /z/), stretch the initial sound for three seconds and have students repeat your model (/lllet/). If the initial sound is not continuous (/b/, /d/, / g/, /h/, /j/, /k/, /p/, /kw/, or /t/), repeat the sound several times (e.g., /b/ /b/ /b/ /at/ rather than /bat/).

3. **Guided Practice** Have students practice finding the word that doesn't belong for more sets of words.

   Now let's try it together. I will say three words. Listen to the beginning sound in each word. Tell me which word doesn't belong.

let, lot, met	**set, let, sad**	**cup, cap, pup**	**log, dog, dad**
red, fell, fan	**nest, rest, not**	**mat, cat, man**	**jet, jam, pet**

4. **Practice** Have students name words with the same initial sound on their own.

   It's your turn. I'll say two words. If they all start with the same sound, repeat the words. Then tell me another word that starts with the same sound.

set, sat	**go, no**	**fun, run**	**bad, bed**
lunch, lamp	**pet, pat**	**dog, dig**	**man, can**

For additional independent practice, students can complete related pages from the **Practice Book** or do Phonological Awareness Activities online. See Additional Strategies and Tips for Teaching Phonological Awareness on page 45 for more ideas.

Phoneme Blending Routine

Introduce this routine by first blending two-letter VC words, such as *am* and *it*. Progress to CVC words that begin with a continuous sound (e.g., /f/, /l/, /m/, /n/, /r/, /s/, /v/, /z/). Next blend words that start with stop sounds (e.g., /b/, /d/, and /g/). Finally, blend words that begin with consonant blends and digraphs. Blending phoneme by phoneme should begin with two-phoneme words at the beginning of Kindergarten, move to three-phoneme words by mid-year, and then to four- or five-phoneme words in Grades 1 and 2.

1. **Explain** Briefly explain the routine and its purpose to students.

   Today we will be blending, or putting together, sounds to make words.

2. **Model** Say each sound in a word. Model how to blend the sounds to make the words.

   I will put sounds together to make a word. Listen: /s/ /a/ /t/, /sssaaat/, sat. The word is sat.

3. **Guided Practice** Have students practice blending words phoneme by phoneme, sound by sound. Do the first word with students.

   Listen to the sounds. Blend, or put together, the sounds to say the whole word.

/s/ /a/ /d/	/m/ /a/ /t/
/l/ /i/ /p/	/r/ /u/ /n/

   Now let's try some harder ones. Listen to the word parts. Blend, or put together, the word parts to say the whole word.

/h/ /a/ /d/	/f/ /l/ /a/ /t/
/w/ /i/ /sh/	/s/ /l/ /i/ /p/
/s/ /p/ /u/ /n/	/f/ /l/ /i/ /p/ /s/

4. **Practice** Students can practice independently by completing related pages from the **Practice Book** or doing Phonological Awareness Activities online. See Additional Strategies and Tips for Teaching Phonological Awareness on page 45 for more ideas for independent practice.

Teaching Tip

A phoneme is an individual sound and can be represented by a single letter, such as *s* for /s/, or by a combination of letters, such as *sh* for /sh/ or *oy* for /oi/.

Corrective Feedback

When students make mistakes during blending, stretch (or sing) the sounds together. Move your hands from right to left as you move from sound to sound to emphasize the changing sounds. Repeat the routine using the same word, asking students to respond without you. Go back and repeat the last two examples before proceeding with additional examples.

Phoneme Segmentation Routine

For this routine, use the Response Board to help students see and feel each sound in the word. You can also use a rubber band to show students how you stretch the sounds in a word.

Introduce the routine by first segmenting two-letter VC words, such as *am* and *it*. Progress to CVC words that begin with a continuous sound (e.g., /f/, /l/, /m/, /n/, /r/, /s/, /v/, /z/). Next, segment words that start with stop sounds (e.g., /b/, /d/, and /g/). Finally, segment words that begin with consonant blends or consonant digraphs. Segmenting phoneme by phoneme should begin with two-phoneme words at the beginning of Kindergarten, move to three-phoneme words by mid-year, and then to four- or five-phoneme words in Grades 1 and 2.

1. **Explain** Briefly explain the routine and its purpose.

   We will be taking apart a word sound by sound.

2. **Model** Provide several models of how to segment the sounds in a word.

   I will say a word, then I will say it sound by sound. As I say each sound, I will place one counter in each box on the Response Board. Listen: sat. Stretch each sound for three seconds so students can hear each discrete sound.

   Now I will say sat *sound by sound.*
   /sss/ Place counter in first box.
   /aaa/ Place counter in second box.
   /t/ Place counter in third box.
   The word sat *has three sounds.* Point to each box as you say: /s/ /a/ /t/.

3. **Guided Practice** Segment the first word with students. Then have students practice segmenting words phoneme by phoneme, or sound by sound, as a group. Once the group has successfully blended a few words, select individual students to take a turn.

   Listen to the sounds. Take apart the word, sound by sound.

sad /s/ /a/ /d/	**mat** /m/ /a/ /t/
fish /f/ /i/ /sh/	**lip** /l/ /i/ /p/
run /r/ /u/ n/	**net** /n/ /e/ t/

Teaching Tip

Although digraphs are spelled with more than one letter, such as *sh* for /sh/ and *oa* for /ō/, they represent only one sound, so only move one counter for each digraph.

Corrective Feedback

If students make mistakes during segmenting, stretch the word using the rubber band technique. Have students repeat. Then use the Response Board to model how to place one counter on each box as you stretch the word and move from sound to sound. Repeat the routine using the same word, asking students to respond without you. Provide immediate feedback, as necessary.

Now let's try some harder ones. Take apart these words, sound by sound.

had /h/ /a/ /d/	**flat** /f/ /l/ /a/ /t/
spun /s/ /p/ /u/ /n/	**flips** /f/ /l/ /i/ /p/ /s/

4. Practice Students can practice independently by completing related pages from the **Practice Book** or doing Phonological Awareness Activities online. See Additional Strategies and Tips for Teaching Phonological Awareness on page 45 for more ideas for independent practice.

Phoneme Deletion Routine

Follow this instructional sequence as you teach students to delete phonemes: 1) initial sounds, 2) final sounds, 3) second letter in a blend, and 4) first letter in a blend.

1. Explain Briefly explain the routine and its purpose.

Today we are taking sounds out of words.

2. Model Provide several models of how to delete a phoneme.

I am going to say a word. Then I will take out the first sound. Listen: mat. If I take out /m/ I get /at/. Let's do another one. Watch. This is the word cat. Show three fingers or tokens. *If I take away the /k/, I have /at/.*

3. Guided Practice Have students practice deleting sounds. Say the word. Then state the position of the sound to be deleted; have students say the new word. Students can use their Response Boards to help them identify the location of the sounds.

Now let's do this together. I will say a word. You will take away the first sound and say a new word.

fat (at)	**sit (it)**	**send (end)**
cup (up)	**gate (ate)**	**boats (oats)**

> **Corrective Feedback**
>
> If students have difficulty, model how to segment the word using the Response Board. Then model the deletion task again, saying the word and running your fingers under the counters, then removing the counter in the target position as you delete the sound.

4. Practice Students can practice independently by completing related pages from the **Practice Book** or doing Phonological Awareness Activities online. See Additional Strategies and Tips for Teaching Phonological Awareness on page 45 for more ideas for independent practice.

Phoneme Substitution Routine

Follow this instructional sequence as you teach students to substitute phonemes: 1) initial sounds, 2) final sounds, 3) medial sounds, 4) second letter in a blend, and 5) first letter in a blend.

1. **Explain** Briefly explain the routine and its purpose.

   Today we will be changing a sound in a word to make a new word.

2. **Model** Provide several models for students. You can use the Response Board to help children locate which sound to change.

   I am going to say a word. Then I will change the first sound to make a new word. Listen: mat. *The first sound is /m/. What is the first sound? /m/ I'm going to change the /m/ to /s/. Now the word is* sat. *Your turn.*

Corrective Feedback

If students make mistakes, model how to find the target sound, remove it, and replace it with the new sound. Have students repeat. Then have students chorally blend the new word formed.

3. **Guided Practice** Have students use their Response Boards to practice substituting sounds. Have them say the word, placing a counter on the board for each sound. Then state the replacement sound and where it should be positioned. Do the first one with students.

   Now let's try it together. I will say a word. I want you to replace the first sound in the word with /s/.

mad (sad)	fell (sell)	hit (sit)
rock (sock)	fun (sun)	bend (send)

4. **Practice** Students can practice independently by completing related pages from the **Practice Book** or doing Phonological Awareness Activities online. See Additional Strategies and Tips for Teaching Phonological Awareness on page 45 for more ideas for independent practice.

Phoneme Addition Routine

1. **Explain** Briefly explain the routine and its purpose.

   Today we will be adding a sound to a word to make a new word.

2. **Model** Provide several models of how to add a phoneme.

   I am going to say a word. Then I will add the sound /s/ at the beginning of it.

   Listen: at. I will add the sound /s/. The new word is sat.

3. **Guided Practice** Have students practice adding sounds. Say the word. Then state the position of the sound to be added.

   Now let's do it together. I will say a word. Add /s/ to the beginning to make a new word.

   | it (sit) | oar (soar) | end (send) | and (sand) |

4. **Practice** Students can practice independently by completing related pages from the **Practice Book** or doing Phonological Awareness Activities online. See Additional Strategies and Tips for Teaching Phonological Awareness on page 45 for more ideas for independent practice.

Corrective Feedback

If students have difficulty, provide additional modeling. Use the Response Board to help students visualize adding a sound.

Phoneme Reversal Routine

1. **Explain** Briefly explain the routine and its purpose.

   Today we will flip the sounds in a word to make a new word.

2. **Model** Provide several models of how to reverse phonemes to form a new word.

   I am going to say a word. Then I will flip the sounds in it. That means I will say the sounds in the reverse order: the last sound becomes first, and the first sound becomes last.

   Listen: top. To flip the sounds, I move the last sound /p/ to the beginning, and the beginning sound /t/ to the end. The new word is pot.

3. **Guided Practice** Have students practice phonemic reversals.

   Now let's try it together. I will say a word. I want you to flip the sounds.

tip (pit)	**net (ten)**	**tap (pat)**
nap (pan)	**team (meat)**	**tell (let)**

4. **Practice** Students can practice independently by completing related pages from the **Practice Book** or doing Phonological Awareness Activities online. See Additional Strategies and Tips for Teaching Phonological Awareness on page 45 for more ideas for independent practice.

Corrective Feedback

Provide additional modeling. Have students say the word and then say what the first sound is. Have them say the word again, and then say what the last sound. Then ask them to flip the sounds.

Additional Strategies for Teaching Phonological and Phonemic Awareness

Independent Practice Options Be sure to model how to do the activities before assigning them to pairs or individual students or placing in centers.

- Do the corresponding Phonemic Awareness Interactive Games and Activities at **my.mheducation.com**.

- Complete corresponding pages in the **Practice Book.**

- Use picture cards and sorting mats to sort rhyming words and categorize initial, final, and medial sounds.

- Use picture cards and the audio recorder to

    - generate rhyming words; words that have the same initial, final, or medial sound; or alliterative phrases and sentences;

    - segment words by syllable, onset and rime, or phoneme by phoneme;

    - manipulate phonemes (substitution, deletion, reversals, addition).

Feel the Rhythm Support students who have difficulty discriminating words in a stream of text by engaging them in kinesthetic activities that get them moving to a beat, such as dancing, drumming, or tapping. Then link the movement to words by having students act out lyrics in a song or tap a drum to the rhythm in a poem or nursery rhyme. Chanting poems or rhymes, stomping or dancing to a beat, or performing action rhymes are also effective ways to boost students' phonological awareness.

Moodboard/Image Source

Name That Sound Select a story that you have recently read aloud to the class. As you read, have students listen for words that contain the consonant or vowel sound you choose. After a minute, pause and ask students to say the words they heard that contain that sound.

Transitions Use transition times to build phonological and phonemic awareness. When you're ready for students to transition from one activity to another, call out a word and have students stop what they are doing and respond with two words that rhyme with it. Then have them move onto the next activity. Alternatively, use transitions to give them practice in hearing the syllables in words. Say a word with more than one syllable. Have them repeat it, clapping for each syllable. Then have them move onto the next activity.

Rhyme Time! Collect pictures of objects with names that can be easily rhymed (e.g., cat, socks, car). Hold up one picture at a time and have students name what the picture shows and then think of as many words as possible that rhyme with it.

Blend It! Slowly say the phonemes in a CVC word. Have students see how quickly they can blend the sounds together. Repeat for several more words. Once students can quickly blend CVC words, do the same activity with words that have more phonemes.

Phonics

What You Need to Know About Phonics

Phonics is the understanding that there is a relationship between sounds (phonemes) and spellings (graphemes). Phonics instruction helps beginning readers understand the relationship between letters and sounds. It teaches students to use these relationships to read and write. Research has shown that direct, systematic phonics instruction is appropriate and beneficial for advancing students' skills from Kindergarten on (NICHD, 2001). When teaching phonics, the sequence of skills can have an impact on students' progress. *Wonders* follows these guidelines for instruction:

- Teach short-vowel sounds (in VC and CVC words) before long-vowel sounds (in CVVC and CVCe words).

- Teach consonants and short vowels in combination so words can be generated as early as possible.

- Be sure the majority of the consonants taught early on are continuous consonants, such as *f, l, m, n, r,* and *s.* These consonant sounds can be stretched, or sustained, without distortion and make it easier to blend words.

- Use a sequence in which the most words can be generated. Teach high-utility letters such as *m, s,* and *t* before lower-utility letters such as *x* or *z.*

- Progress from simple to more complex sound-spellings. For example, single consonants should be taught before consonant blends and digraphs. Likewise, short vowels should be taught before long vowels, variant vowels, and diphthongs.

- Separate visually and auditorially confusing letters and sounds (e.g., *m/n, e/i, b/d*) in the instructional sequence.

> **❝ Learning phonics is a cumulative process. Students learn new letter sounds and then use them to decode words. Those learned sounds then serve as a foundation as students continue to learn new sounds and incorporate them to expand their decoding repertoire. Students learn new sounds while continually reviewing and practicing decoding with previously learned sounds. Decoding is mastered through this iterative process. ❞**
>
> **— Dr. Jan Hasbrouck**

Research

- Phonics instruction has a positive overall effect on reading and can benefit students of all levels.
- Phonics instruction has positive overall effects on specific skill areas including decoding, spelling, reading orally, and comprehending text.
- Phonics instruction has a lasting impact on reading. It should always be connected to reading and writing practice.
- Phonics instruction is best when it is explicit and systematic, done early, and done well. The majority of phonics instruction occurs in Grades K–2, but work continues on less-common patterns, syllabication, affixes, and Greek and Latin roots well into the upper elementary years.
- Phonics and spelling instruction are interrelated processes, and instruction should be linked.
- Using decodable texts in early reading accelerates students' knowledge and use of phonics patterns, improves their spelling, and positively affects their motivation to read (Blevins, 2000).

How Does *Wonders* Teach Phonics?

Phonics instruction begins in the first unit in Kindergarten with explicit instruction in letter recognition and letter-sound relationships. Throughout the Kindergarten year, children learn letter names and sounds and have multiple opportunities to apply them daily in whole- and small-group lessons. All consonants and short and long vowel sounds are taught and practiced in Kindergarten, using materials such as

- Alphabet Teaching Poster
- Word-Building Cards
- Pre-Decodable Stories
- Practice Book Pages
- Decodable Stories
- Big Books
- Sound-Spelling Cards
- Response Boards
- Letter Cards
- Letter Songs
- Interactive Games and Activities

Phonics instruction continues in Grades 1 and 2 with daily systematic and explicit whole- and small-group lessons that are linked to phonemic awareness, spelling, and handwriting instruction each week. The target sound is introduced through a phonemic awareness lesson, then the sound-spelling relationship is taught. Students apply their learning in decodable readers, practice building and blending words with the target skill, and work with spelling words containing the target sound-spelling. In Grades 3 and up, a weekly phonics lesson helps students decode multisyllabic words and is integrated with reading instrution.

Throughout the grades, phonics instruction is variable and based on students' needs as determined by assessments. Daily Quick Check Observations in Grades K–2 and weekly assessments in all grades help teachers determine the needs for differentiated phonics instruction; in K–2, Small Group options (Approaching, On-Level) are provided to meet students' specific instructional needs.

What Does Success Look Like?

Students know the sounds that letters represent, and they can blend sounds together to make words. They know how to try different sounds if the first attempt doesn't yield a known word, using resources such as the Sound-Spelling Cards as necessary. They can break apart words into syllables, sound out each part, and then blend the parts together. They can identify prefixes, suffixes, base words, and word families to help them decode words. They can also apply their knowledge of syllable patterns to decode words.

Routines

The routines in this section are integrated within the lessons in the **Teacher's Edition.**

Phonics Routine

- Sound-by-Sound Blending
- Sound-Spelling Cards
- Building Words
- Reading Decodables
- Multisyllabic Words
- Reading Big Words

Sound-by-Sound Blending Routine

For each week of phonics instruction in K–2, you will find word lists online to use with the blending routine. For most of the word lists

- Lines 1–2 contain decodable words found in the upcoming selections;
- Line 3 contains minimal contrasts;
- Line 4 contains a mixed list with cumulative review words;
- Lines 5–7 contain sentences.

1. **Explain** Briefly explain the routine and its purpose.

   Today we will be blending sounds to make words. The more practice we have sounding out words with the letters and spellings we have learned, the better readers we will be.

2. **Model** Display the first word, writing it on the Response Board or placing letter cards in a pocket chart. Model how to blend sounds.

   We will say each sound. Watch me, my turn: [Touch under each letter and say the sound]. */s/ /a/ /t/ Now do it with me.* [Touch under each letter and say the sound with students.] *Now do it by yourselves.* [Touch under each letter as students say the sound.]

   Now we will blend the sounds to make a word. Watch me, my turn: [**Point** to the left of *s* and sweep under the *a*, stretching each sound for 1–1 ½ seconds as you blend them.] *Now do it with me.* [Sweep under the letters and blend the sounds with students.] *Now do it by yourselves.* [Sweep under the letters as students say the sound.] Repeat to blend the third sound.

Now we will say the word. Watch me, my turn: [Slide your hand under the word] sat. *Now do it with me.* [Sweep under the letters and say the word with students.] *Now do it by yourselves.* [Sweep under the letters as students say the word.]

Repeat until students understand the task.

3. **Guided Practice** Select words from the list, display them, and have students blend sounds. This portion of the lesson should be brief and take 5–10 minutes maximum.

[**Point** to each letter.] *Sound?* Have students chorally say the sound. Repeat for each letter.

[**Point** to the left of the word; sweep under the first two letters.] *Blend?* Have students chorally blend the sounds. Repeat for all letters in the word.

[**Point** to the left of the word; sweep quickly under the whole word.] *Word?* Have students chorally say the word.

4. **Practice** Provide individual turns as a check. Call on several students for one word each. Call on students in an unpredictable order. Call more frequently on students who made errors.

Have students chorally read the word lists and sentences. Students should read a word every two seconds. This will help to develop fluency with the words and spelling patterns before students read the Decodable Text.

For additional independent practice, assign the corresponding page(s) in the Practice Book or Phonics Activities online. See Additional Strategies for Teaching Phonics on pages 59 and 60 for more ideas.

Corrective Feedback

To correct students who make a **sound error**, model the sound they missed, then have them repeat the sound. If they still make an error, have them say it with you. Take note of those sounds children consistently miss and provide needs-based reteach lessons during small group time.

To correct students who make a **blending error**, model blending again, then lead students in blending, responding with them to offer support. Have them repeat on their own, checking at each blending step. Have them do this once more on their own. Then back up two words and repeat the Guided Practice steps, restate the missed word, and continue on.

If students struggle reading CVC words, use vowel-first blending. Point to the vowel, say its sound, and have children repeat. Then blend the word from the beginning.

Teaching Tip

After months of blending practice, transition students to sounding out words in their head. Follow the same steps in Guided Practice, but have students say the sound in their head only. For the last step, when you sweep under the entire word and prompt students with *Word?*, have them say the word aloud. Be sure to offer enough time for students to blend the word in their heads before saying it, and reinforce this kind of blending when students are reading decodable text. The ultimate goal of blending is Whole Word Reading, where they scan and say the word. When students get to this stage, you may need to remind them they don't have to work through every sound for familiar words.

Sound-Spelling Card

Sound-Spelling Cards Routine

The Sound-Spelling Cards are a set of 47 full-color cards for the most frequently taught sounds. The front of each card shows the letter or letters that most commonly represent the sound, a familiar image to help students link the sound to a word containing it, and spelling variations of the sound. The back of each Sound-Spelling Card offers additional teaching support. See the Sound-Spelling Cards User's Guide at **my.mheducation.com** for more details.

1. **Explain** Briefly name and explain the task and its purpose.

   Today we will learn a new sound-spelling.

2. **Model** Teach the target sound. Show the Sound-Spelling Card. State the name of the letter(s) and say the sound the letter(s) represent. Then attach the sound to the name of the image shown in the picture on the front of the card. Point out the spelling(s) you will focus on; write each spelling as you say the sound.

   This is the Ss *Sound-Spelling Card. The sound is /s/. The /s/ sound is spelled with the letter* s. *Say it with me: /s/. This is the sound at the beginning of the word* sun. [**Point** *to picture on card.*] *Watch as I write the letter* s. *I will say the sound /s/ as I write the letter.*

   Point out any color-coding or hints on the cards, which include

   - cards with dotted borders represent sounds that transfer from Spanish to English;
   - cards with solid borders represent sounds that do not transfer from Spanish to English;
   - a red box before a spelling (e.g., __dge) represents that the spelling follows a short vowel sound;
   - a line within or after the spelling (e.g., a_e, gi_) signals that a consonant is missing.

3. **Guided Practice** Have students practice connecting the sound and spelling through writing.

   Now do it with me. Say /s/ as I write the letter.

   This time, write the letter s *five times as you say the /s/ sound.*

4. **Practice** Help students build fluency by reviewing the sound-spellings you have taught using the Word-Building Cards. Maintain a set of cards representing the sound-spellings taught. Display one card at a time as students chorally say the sound. Then mix up the cards and repeat at a faster pace. Spend no more than 2–3 minutes on this practice.

Let's review the spellings we have learned so far. Look at the spelling on the Word Building Card. Say the sound. [Go through all the cards.]

Now it's time for the speed challenge. Let's see how quickly we can say the sounds.

Remember, knowing these sound-spellings quickly and accurately will help us sound out words as we read.

Building Words Routine

This routine gives students practice manipulating sounds and spelling. Start by changing initial sound-spellings. Progress to changing final sound spellings. Then change medial vowel spellings.

1. **Explain** Briefly name and explain the task and its purpose.

   Today we will be building, or making, words using the letters and spellings we have learned.

2. **Model** Place Word-Building Cards in a pocket chart to form the first word you are building. Model blending the phonemes. Then replace a card with a different one, blend the sounds, and say the new word.

   [Place cards *f, e,* and *d* in a pocket chart.] *Look at the word I have made. It is spelled* f-e-d. *Listen as I blend the sounds, then read the word: /fffeeed/,* fed. *Your turn. Blend. Read.*

   Repeat with two more words with the target sound-spelling.

3. **Guided Practice** Give children a set of Word-Building Cards containing all the sound-spellings for your list of words. Have them build the last word you modeled with, then change one or more letters in the word. Have children chorally blend the new word formed. Do a set of at least ten words.

   Build the word red. *Now change* r *to* l. *What is the new word? Let's blend the sounds and read the word: /llleeed/,* led.

   Change d *to* g. *What is the new word? Let's blend the sounds and read the word: /llleeeg/,* leg.

   Continue with words *beg, bet, bat, mat, met, men, pen, pan, pat, pet.*

4. **Practice** For independent practice, assign the corresponding page(s) in the Practice Book or Phonics Activities online. See Additional Strategies for Teaching Phonics on pages 59 and 60 for more ideas.

> **Teaching Tip**
>
> This portion of the lesson should be quick and take no more than two minutes.

> **Corrective Feedback**
>
> If students make mistakes during word building, model blending the new word formed.

> **Teaching Tip**
>
> For variety, ask students to change a sound in a word. For example, say *Change the first sound in* sat *to /m/. What new word will you make?*

Reading Decodables Routine

Decodable Readers provide an excellent opportunity for students to apply their skills of word reading to connected text.

1. **Review High-Frequency Words** Display the High-Frequency Word Cards for the words in the text. Use the Read/Spell/Write Routine to review (see page 63).

2. **Preview and Predict** Read the title aloud. Ask students what they see. For English learners, describe the first page using academic language first. Then ask students what they think will happen in the text. Use prompts such as the following:

   Where are the characters? What are they doing?
   Why do you think they are doing that?
   What do you think might happen next?

3. **First Read (Together)** Read the story chorally with students. Have students point to each word, sounding out the decodable words and saying the high-frequency words quickly.

4. **Check Comprehension** Ask questions that focus on overall comprehension; you'll find questions for the Decodable Readers in the **Teacher's Edition** lessons. During this step

   - prompt students to answer in complete sentences;
   - have students point to sentences that support their answers;
   - have partners discuss a question together;
   - lead a discussion of any difficult words from the selection.

5. **Second Read (Build Fluency)** Have students reread the book, using this time to differentiate instruction and practice:

   - Chorally reread the book with Approaching and On-Level students.
   - If students struggle to sound out decodable words, model blending them. Then review blending using the list at the end of the reader during small group time. Then reread the book.
   - Have Beyond Level students read the text with a partner. They should read alternating pages. Have the reader point to each word as the listener follows in his or her book. Students then switch roles. Finally, have partners retell the story to each other.

6. **Cumulative Review** Have students reread the current week's decodable stories and as many previous stories as time allows.

Corrective Feedback

If students do not read a decodable word correctly, model how to sound out the word using the blending routine. Repeat the routine with the same word, having students blend the sounds with you. Then go back to the beginning of the sentence and read each word with students.

Multisyllabic Words Routine

1. **Explain** Remind students that a syllable has one vowel sound, although that sound may be represented by more than one letter. Breaking a word into syllables can help students decode it. Introduce or review the lesson's target syllable pattern.

   Closed Syllables end in a consonant. The vowel is "closed in" by the consonants and the sound is usually short. (rab/bit)

   Open Syllables end in a vowel. The vowel sound is usually long; the vowel is open and free to say its name. (si/lo)

   Consonant + *le* Syllables When a word ends in *le*, the consonant that precedes it plus the letters *le* form the final syllable. (han/dle)

   Vowel Team/Digraph Syllables In vowel digraphs, the vowels act as a team and must remain in the same syllable. (crea/ture)

   ***r*-Controlled Vowel Syllables** When a vowel is followed by the letter *r*, the vowel and *r* must remain in the same syllable. (tur/tle)

   Final *e* (Silent *e*) Syllables When a word ends in *e*, often the vowel before it and the letter *e* act as a team to form the vowel sound and must therefore remain in the same syllable. (be/have)

2. **Model** Model using the target syllable pattern to decode a word.

   [Display the word *table*.] *I notice that this word ends with* le; *that's one of the main syllable types. The consonant that comes before the* le *is part of the syllable, so I will break the word before the* b. [Draw a line between the *a* and the *b*.] *The first part ends with a vowel; it's an open syllable, so I'll try the long vowel sound first: / tā/ /bəl/. When I blend those sounds, I get* table, *a word I know.*

3. **Guided Practice** Write words containing the target syllable type on the board. Have students underline the target syllable type in each word. Then guide them to sound out the syllables and blend the syllables into a word. Have students chorally read the words. Next, give partners Word-Building Cards and have them build words containing the target syllable type.

4. **Practice** Engage students in regular practice reading multisyllabic words with the following activities:

   - Completing pages in the Practice Book
   - Reading Decodable Texts
   - Doing Speed Drills
   - Writing words that contain the target syllable pattern

Teaching Tip

Review previously taught syllable types as necessary, especially open and closed syllables to help students choose which type of vowel sound to try first. Closed syllables typically have a short vowel sound, while open syllables usually have a long vowel sound.

Reading Big Words Routine

1. **Explain** Tell students you will be teaching them a strategy for decoding long words.

2. **Model** Model the five-step strategy:

   Step 1: Look for word parts (prefixes) at the beginning of the word.

   [Write the word *rebuilding* on the board. Do not pronounce the word.] *When we come across a word we don't know, the first step is to look at the beginning and check for any word parts we know. These parts are prefixes.* [Prompt students to name prefixes they know.] *When I look at this word, I see the prefix "re," which I know means "again." So I know how this word begins.*

   Step 2: Look for word parts (suffixes) at the end of the word.

   Then I look at the end of the word. That's where we might find a suffix. [Review the definition of suffixes as necessary and prompt students to name suffixes they know.] *I see the suffix "ing" at the end of this word. I know that part is added to a verb to show an action that is happening now. So I know how the word ends.*

   Step 3: In the base word, look for familiar spelling patterns. Think about the six syllable-spelling patterns you have learned.

   Now I look at what's left. This is called the base word. I check if I know it. In this case, I do: build. *If I didn't know it, I would look for spelling patterns that I know and think about the syllable patterns I know to help me decode the word.*

   Step 4: Sound out and blend together the word.

   Now we put the word parts together and blend them. Let's say it together: re-build-ing.

Step 5: Say the word parts quickly. Adjust your pronunciation as needed. Ask yourself: "Is it a real word?" "Does it make sense in the sentence?"

Now let's say the word parts quickly: rebuilding. *That's a word I have heard before. I knew they were rebuilding the homes destroyed by the earthquake. Using the word parts I can also figure out what the word means. Since* re *means again, I can figure out that* rebuilding *means "building again."*

3. **Guided Practice** Give students a copy of the Decoding Strategy Chart. Review the steps with them. Then give them a set of multisyllabic words with which to practice the strategy.

4. **Practice** Post the Decoding Strategy Chart (see page 58) in the classroom and have students keep a copy in their writer's notebook. Encourage students to use the strategy whenever they come across a long word they don't know.

Corrective Feedback

If students struggle to identify prefixes and suffixes, offer immediate support, then review these during small group time.

If students have difficulty identifying the base word, guide them to use their knowledge of syllable patterns to decode.

Decoding Strategy Chart

Step 1	Look for word parts (prefixes) at the beginning of the word.
Step 2	Look for word parts (suffixes) at the end of the word.
Step 3	In the base word, look for familiar spelling patterns. Think about the six syllable-spelling patterns you have learned.
Step 4	Sound out and blend together the word parts.
Step 5	Say the word parts fast. Adjust your pronunciation as needed. Ask yourself: "Is this a word I have heard before?" Then read the word in the sentence and ask: "Does it make sense in this sentence?"

Additional Strategies for Teaching Phonics

Practice Options Provide fast-paced, fun, daily practice.

- **Blending Practice:** Select five words with the current week's sound-spelling and five words with previously taught sound-spellings. Guide student to blend each word sound by sound, then chorally read all the words.
- **Speed Drills:** Use the Word-Building Cards to review sound-spellings. Use a stopwatch to time how long it takes the class to chorally read a set of cards and challenge them to beat their time.
- **Sound-Spelling Songs:** Use the online videos to teach students movements and songs to help them remember sound-spellings.

Independent Practice Ideas These can be done as center activities, with partners, or independently. Be sure to model how to do the activities before assigning them.

- **Phonics Interactive Games and Activities:** Assign targeted practice from the resources at **my.mheducation.com**.
- **Practice Book:** Assign the corresponding pages.
- **Word-Building Challenge:** Have students use Word-Building Cards to generate words with the target spelling and/or syllable pattern and record lists in their writer's notebook.
- **Word Hunts:** Have students search for words with a target sound-spelling pattern in their writer's notebooks, independent reading materials, or other resources.
- **Word Sorts:** Have students sort words by target sound-spelling patterns. Begin with closed sorts, giving students categories and having them sort the words. Then give students words and have them determine categories and sort the words. Once students have sorted a group of words several times, challenge them to do a speed-sort and see how quickly they can sort the words. See pages 69–70 for sorting routines.

Use a Pointer Use a fun pointer to tap under words as you read aloud text to and with students to help them develop the concept of a word. Print rhymes, songs, or poems on chart paper or display on a whiteboard for this purpose. Once students have memorized the words, invite individuals to come up and use the pointer to point to the words as the class chants or sings. In small group, give each student an individual pointer (as simple as an eraser or cotton swab and as creative as you wish) and have them point to words on their copy of a familiar text as the group reads or chants chorally.

Small-Group Word Lists Use the lists on the back of the Sound-Spelling Cards for phonemic awareness activities, word-building practice, and decoding exercises during small group time.

Create Personal Readers As you read and teach poems, songs, and rhymes with Beginning readers, make copies of the text for students and put them in a three-ring binder or folder. Number and date each text and keep them in order. Give students time each day to reread the texts, building their automaticity. They can also take the readers home and reread to caregivers for extra practice.

Partner Reading Have children reread selections from the week's Leveled Reader, Differentiated Genre Passage, or their Personal Reader with a partner.

Use Word Study Notebooks Give each student a notebook devoted to word study. The word study notebook can serve as a record of word sorts and word hunts in addition to vocabulary activities such as word squares. It's also a good place for students to write reflections on what they've learned through their word study activities.

High-Frequency Words

What You Need to Know About High-Frequency Words

High-frequency words are the most common words in the English language. The high-frequency words taught in *Wonders* are derived from established word lists, such as the *Dolch Basic Sight Vocabulary* list of the top 220 words (no nouns), the Fry top 100 words, and the *American Heritage Word Frequency Book* top 150 words in printed school English. Some of the high-frequency words in English must be taught as sight words because they do not follow regular sound-spelling patterns, such as *said, come,* and *who.*

Because these words are so common in English school text, mastery of these words is necessary to fluent reading. Many of these words trip up struggling readers (such as words that begin with *th* and *wh*) and can impede comprehension when incorrectly identified during reading.

> ❝A majority of the words students will encounter are repeated frequently. When students can instantaneously recognize these high frequency words, their comprehension improves because they can focus on the meaning of the text. Helping students acquire a large body of deeply memorized words makes reading effective and motivating. ❞
>
> – Dr. Jan Hasbrouck

Research

- High-frequency words make up a significant portion of the words students need to read and write. In fact, 25% of all words and print come from this set of thirteen words: *a, and, for, he, is, in, it, of, that, the, to, was, you* (Johns, 1981). And about 50% of words students will read and write come from a set of 100 words (Fry, Fountoukidis, & Polk, 1985).

- Many high-frequency words do not follow common sound-spelling patterns, so they need to be learned by sight and require explicit instruction.

How Does *Wonders* Teach High-Frequency Words?

To really "know" a word, the word's sound, meaning, and spelling patterns (all activated in separate parts of the brain) must be internalized. The most effective instructional strategy to facilitate this is the **Read/Spell/Write Routine**; see below. In addition, students need to practice reading the words in connected text. In early Kindergarten, *Wonders* provides pre-decodable texts comprised of high-frequency words that students have learned, using rebus or picture clues for words students are not able to decode. These texts build word automaticity with taught high-frequency words and serve as excellent instructional tools for practicing book handling and developing concepts of print. In later Kindergarten and beyond, high-frequency words are built into the Shared Read, Paired Selections, Anchor Texts, Leveled Readers, and Differentiated Genre Passages, offering many opportunities for students to build fluency with these words. Word Work lessons also incorporate high-frequency word practice and review.

Ideally, students will have automaticity with the top 300 high-frequency words by the time they enter the third grade, but some students in Grades 3 and beyond will still need instruction and practice to gain fluency with these words. Approaching Level lessons in the **Teacher's Edition** teach and review a small set of high-frequency words each week. In addition, you can find High-Frequency Speed Drills and Fluency Phrase Charts on the Tier 2 Fluency Teacher's Guides online.

What Does Success Look Like?

Students can read high-frequency words automatically when they see them in text.

Routines

The routines in this section are integrated into the Word Work lessons in the **Teacher's Edition.**

High-Frequency Words Routines

- Read/Spell/Write
- Reading Pre-Decodable Texts

Read/Spell/Write Routine

Remind students that high-frequency words are important to know automatically since they appear so often in text. Since they often do not follow regular sound-spelling patterns or contain sound-spelling students have not yet learned, students need to memorize the words by sight. Display the list of high-frequency words you wish to teach or review and guide students through this routine.

1. **Read** *This is the word* said. *Say it with me:* said. *My friend said she was hungry.*

2. **Spell** *The word* said *is spelled* s-a-i-d. *Spell it with me:* s-a-i-d.

   Briefly point out any spelling patterns students have learned to help them distinguish the word from other similar words and to ensure that students fully analyze the word.

   What's the first sound you hear in said? (/s/) What letter have we learned for the /s/ sound? (s)

   Repeat for any other known sound-spellings in the word.

3. **Write** Have students write the word multiple times as they spell it aloud.

   Your turn. Read the word, then write the word five times. Spell it aloud as you write it.

> ### Teaching Tip
>
> You can also have children write the word in the air as they say each letter.

Reading Pre-Decodable Texts Routine

Teaching Tip

If rebuses are used in the text, review the illustrations with students. This portion of the lesson should be quick and take no more than two minutes.

1. **Review High-Frequency Words** Display the High-Frequency Word Cards for the words in the text. Use the Read/Spell/Write Routine to review (see page 63).

2. **Preview and Predict** Read the title aloud. Then point to each word and have the students chorally read the title with you. Ask students to discuss what they see on the cover. For English learners, describe the cover using academic language prior to asking them about the cover's contents. Then ask students what they think will happen in the story. Use prompts such as the following to help children think about the text.

   Where are the characters? What are they doing?

   How do they feel? How do you know?

   Why do you think they are doing that?

   What do you think might happen next?

Corrective Feedback

Choral Reading: If a student does not read a word correctly, model how to read the word using the Read/Spell/Write Routine (see page 63). Then read the sentence again from the beginning with students.

3. **First Read (Read Together)** Turn to the first page of the Pre-Decodable Text and read the story chorally with students. Have students point to each word, saying the high-frequency words quickly.

4. **Check Comprehension** Ask questions that focus on overall comprehension; you'll find questions for the texts in the **Teacher's Edition** lessons. During this step:

   - Prompt students to answer in complete sentences.
   - Have students point to sentences in the story that support their answers.
   - Have partners discuss at least one question together before sharing with the group.
   - Lead a discussion of any difficult words from the selection.

Corrective Feedback

Provide sentence starters to help partners provide feedback:

- The word is _____.
- Let's say the word together, _____.
- Now let's read the sentence again.

5. **Second Read (Fluency)** Have students reread the book with a partner. One partner reads the book in its entirety as the listener follows along by pointing to each word read. Then partners switch roles. Circulate, listen in, and provide corrective feedback as necessary.

6. **Cumulative Review** As time allows, have students reread the current week's pre-decodable stories and as many previous stories as possible.

Additional Strategies for Teaching High-Frequency Words

High-Frequency Word Cards Each grade has a set of high-frequency word cards available online. Use these for quick reviews of current and past high-frequency words, with the whole class or in small group. You can also give students their own set of cards. Have them write a meaningful sentence or phrase on the back of the card and practice reading the word and the sentence/phrase with a partner.

Speed Drills In small group, display the high-frequency word cards in succession. Use a stopwatch to time how long is takes the group to chorally read a set of cards. Then challenge students to beat the time. This can also be a center activity where students time themselves. You can find Speed Drills for high-frequency words in the Tier 2 Fluency Teacher's Guide online.

High-Frequency Phrase Drills Use the high-frequency phrase drills from the Tier 2 Fluency Teacher's Guide online to give students more practice reading high-frequency words.

Mix It Fix It For extra practice during small group, take one or more high-frequency word(s) students are studying and make individual letter cards so each word can be spelled. Place the letter cards in random order and secure them with paper clips; make a set for each student in the group. Use the following steps:

- Have students lay out the letter cards and say the letter names. (**HINT:** Draw a line on the bottom of the letter to identify the direction that the letter card should be placed on the table.)
- Say the high-frequency word and have students spell it with the letter cards. You can give them hints, or even write the word on a white board and hold it up for them to see the letters and their order for the word.
- Have students slide each letter up and say the letter name. (For example: "a-w-a-y." Then have them read the word to a partner or to you.
- Tell students to "mix" the letters back up and have them re-create ("fix") the word back together several times. Have students write the word on a whiteboard or in their writer's notebook for extra practice.

Spelling

What You Need to Know About Spelling

Spelling is a key component of literacy instruction. Effective spelling instruction teaches students about phonics, vocabulary, and morphology, giving them a deeper understanding of word structure than reading instruction alone. Spelling skills also act as a link between students' oral vocabulary and their writing ability.

> 66 Differentiated word study instruction makes it possible for students to make generalizations about how words are spelled that they use in their reading, writing, and spelling. Developmental word knowledge research clearly outlines a sequence of instruction that matches what principles students need to know about the three layers of English: alphabet, pattern, and meaning. 99
>
> – Dr. Donald Bear

Research

- An analysis of research commissioned by the NRC claimed that spelling instruction—in particular, at the second-grade level—is important in building "phonemic awareness and knowledge of basic letter-sound correspondences" (Snow, Burns, & Griffin, 1998, p. 212).

- "When students sort words, they are engaged in the active process of searching, comparing, contrasting, and analyzing. Word sorts help students organize what they know about words and to form generalizations that they can then apply to new words they encounter in their reading (Gillet & Kita, 1979)" (Bear, Invernizzi, Templeton, & Johnston, 2008).

How Does *Wonders* Teach Spelling?

In *Wonders*, spelling instruction is linked to phonemic awareness and phonics instruction to accelerate students' mastery of the phonics patterns in reading and writing. Each week you will find differentiated spelling lists that feature words containing the sounds and sound-spellings students study during word work lessons in Kindergarten through Grade 2. In Grades 3 and up, a weekly phonics/fluency lesson highlights patterns found in the week's spelling lists. Each week's list also includes review words from the previous week and high-frequency words. All students work with their word lists in hands-on activities, including sorting, differentiated practice pages in the Practice Book, and online activities. The lists are introduced with the Dictation Routine, and students can practice using the Look-Say-Cover-Write-Check Routine and the Open Sort and Closed Sort Routines.

> 66 *Wonders* embeds spelling instruction within word study and differentiates spelling instruction so that it accommodates a wide range of learners, from special needs to gifted students. This approach allows students to investigate and understand the patterns in words, engage in various word sorts, and discover words in meaningful, transferable ways, rather than memorizing disconnected word lists. 99
>
> — **Kathy Bumgardner**

What Does Success Look Like?

Success in spelling can be evaluated in a variety of ways, including the following:

- Satisfactory performance on the weekly spelling test.
- Proficient sorting of words with spelling patterns, specifically
  - **Accuracy:** Accuracy in establishing categories
  - **Fluency:** Speed in categorizing and sorting words
  - **Reflection:** Ability to reflect on the categories
  - **Transfer:** Ability to apply and transfer from word study/spelling to writing and reading.
- Correct spelling of words with target spelling patterns in students' own writing.

Routines

The spelling routines can be used each week with the differentiated spelling lists. Students perform the same tasks using their leveled sets of words.

> ### Spelling Routines
>
> - Dictation
> - Close Sort
> - Open Sort
> - Look-Say-Cover-Write-Check

Dictation Routine

Teach students to use this routine to sound out new spelling words. When you introduce the list at the beginning of the week, read aloud each word and the sample sentence; allow time for students to work through the routine and write the word before continuing to the next one on the list. Model each step and offer time for students to practice before having them use the routine independently.

1. **Say the word.** You may have students chorally say the word after you say it and use it in a simple context sentence (provided in the **Teacher's Edition**).

   > **Has**. *Jim has a pet cat. Say the word with me:* **has**.

2. **Orally segment the word.** Have students say the word sound-by-sound. For multisyllabic words, have students say/clap the word syllable by syllable, and then segment each syllable. (See the Phoneme Segmentation Routine on page 40 for more details.)

   Let's listen to each sound in the word and count them. Has. /h/ /a/ /s/ I hear three sounds.

3. **Connect each sound to a spelling.** Guide students to connect each sound in the word or syllable to a spelling. Refer to the Sound-Spelling Cards as needed.

   What is the first sound? What letter (or letters) do we write for that sound?

4. **Check spelling.** Have students read the word and ask themselves if it looks right. Then display the correct spelling of the word so students can self-correct.

Teaching Tip

Allow students to use Sound Boxes to help them segment the sounds.

Corrective Feedback

If students have an error, refer them to the Sound-Spelling Cards. You can also associate the word to a known word with the same spelling pattern to help students make a connection.

Closed Sort Routine

Closed Sorts are teacher-directed sorts in which you define the categories and model the sorting. Sorting words into categories helps students recognize similar spelling patterns among words. Give students a set of word cards containing the spelling words and the spelling patterns (available at **my.mheducation.com**).

1. **Explain** Briefly explain the task and its purpose.

   Today we will sort our spelling words into categories so it's easier for us to recognize the different spelling patterns.

2. **Model** Display the different spelling patterns students will use to sort. Then demonstrate the following steps with a set of spelling word cards.

   - Hold up a spelling word card.
   - Read the word. Have students blend the sounds together chorally.
   - Spell the word and identify the spelling pattern.
   - Place the word card under the corresponding spelling pattern.
   - Repeat for the other spelling words.

   When the words are sorted, have students read the words in each column with you.

3. **Guided Practice** Have students perform the sort with their set of word cards. Remove the word cards you used but leave the spelling patterns displayed. For each word

   - Hold up the word card.
   - Read and spell the word.
   - Have students chorally repeat the word and its spelling.
   - Have students sort the word card by its spelling pattern.

4. **Practice** Partners can work together to sort the words throughout the week. You may have them

   - Repeat the sort as a center activity.
   - Record the sort in their writer's notebook.
   - Write a reflection about the activity in their writer's notebook.
   - Use the week's words in an Open Sort (see below).

Open Sort Routine

Open Sorts, or student-centered sorts, are sorts in which students create their own categories. Periodically ask students to sort words in any way the choose to check their understanding of spelling patterns. For example, if students continue to sort only by the first letter—ignoring, for example, a common vowel spelling patterns—then they need more instruction and practice in identifying spelling patterns and sorting words. Give students a set of word cards to sort.

1. **Explain** Briefly explain the task and its purpose.

   We're going to sort these words by spelling patterns that we notice. You will decide how to sort them.

2. **Model** Demonstrate how to analyze the words for spelling patterns and group words with the same pattern together.

   Looking through these words, I see pay *and* say *both have the* a-y *spelling pattern. Let's group them together.*

3. **Guided Practice** Have partners work together to sort the rest of the words. As you circulate, ask students to explain their reasoning for grouping the words. When students finish, have them share their sorts and explain their thinking, with another partnership, a small group, or the class.

   Now it's your turn. Work with your partner to decide how to sort the words. Be sure you can explain your thinking.

4. **Practice** Offer opportunities for students to do open sorts regularly. They can

   - Do sorts as a center activity.
   - Record sorts in their writer's notebook.
   - Write a reflection about the sort in their writer's notebook.

Look-Say-Cover-Write-Check Routine

Use this routine developed and adapted by the North Coast Learning Institute to help students practice their spelling words. Model the routine and have students practice together before assigning it independently.

1. **Look** Students look at the word.
2. **Say** Students say the word aloud.
3. **Cover** Students cover the word.
4. **Write** Students write the word without looking at it.
5. **Check** Students check against the original. Pairs can check each other's work.

Additional Strategies for Teaching Spelling

Differentiate Spelling Instruction Use the Inventories of Developmental Spelling in the Placement and Diagnostic Assessment resource (available online) to assess students' spelling stage and differentiate instruction. Inventories are available for Primary (K–3), Elementary (1–6), and Upper Level (6–8). They can be administered whole class and provide detailed information about the spelling stages of students. Then form groups and use the Differentiated Spelling list associated with each group's level. See the Placement and Diagnostic Assessment book for details on administering and using the inventories.

Focus on the Meaning of Words in Context Ensure students understand the meaning of spelling words with activities such as the following. Be sure to introduce and model activities before having partners or individuals work on them independently.

- **Match Definitions to Spelling Words** Provide a list of words in one column and definitions in random order in another, and have students match each word to its definition.
- **Create Analogies** Have students create analogies with their spelling words.
- **Identify Synonyms and Antonyms** Have students generate synonyms and antonyms for spelling words.
- **Use Words in Sentences** Have students write sentences using spelling words that show their meaning.

Offer Practice Opportunities Help students practice their words daily and become familiar with spelling patterns with activities such as the following. Be sure to introduce and model activities before having partners or individuals work on them independently.

- **Word Sorts** In addition to the open and closed sorts described above, incorporate the following sorts:
  - **Speed Sorts** Students can use a stopwatch to time themselves as they do sorts, challenging themselves to improve their time on subsequent sorts.
  - **Blind Sorts** One partner lays down a word card from each category as a header and then reads the rest of the words aloud. The other partner indicates under which header each word goes without seeing the word. The reading partner places the word card under the header the listening partner indicates; the listening partner moves the word if it is placed in the wrong category. Then partners switch roles.
  - **Writing Sort** One student calls out the spelling words in random order. The rest of the group members write them,

putting the words into categories by spelling pattern. Students compare their categories, check their spellings, and repeat with a different student calling out the words.

- **Word Hunts** After students are familiar with a set of spelling patterns, have them search texts they are reading for words with those patterns. Give them a key word for each spelling pattern with the pattern highlighted (written in another color, underlined, etc.). You can assign a text, have students choose texts they are reading independently, or have them search through their own writing. Students can record the Word Hunts in their writer's notebook.

- **Word Study Games** Almost any card game can be adapted for word study.
  - **"Go Fish" Card Game:** Using the Spelling Word Cards, students match cards with similar spelling patterns. The student with the most pairs wins.
  - **Concentration:** Provide a set of word cards with duplicates of each spelling word. Have students shuffle the cards and place them face-side down in rows. Students take turns turning over cards to find two words that match. The student with the most cards wins.
  - **Board Game:** For each space on the board, write a word with a spelling pattern students have studied. The first player draws from a stack of Spelling Word Cards. The player reads the words and moves to the first square containing a word with the same spelling pattern.

- **Online Spelling Activities** Have students do the online spelling activities.

- **Practice Book** Have students complete the differentiated Practice Book page that corresponds to their list.

Introduce Activities in Small Groups Introducing word study activities in small groups enables you to monitor students' understanding and assess their ability to complete a task independently. It also allows you to scaffold students as they learn how to complete the activity and gives you insight into their developmental spelling level.

Encourage Reflection Teach students to reflect on their learning orally and in their writer's notebooks. You can provide prompts such as:

- When sorting words today, I noticed . . .
- This activity helped me learn . . .
- When I'm not sure how to spell a word, I can . . .

Vocabulary

What You Need to Know About Vocabulary

Vocabulary is the knowledge of words and their meanings. Vocabulary development focuses on words beyond basic sight words. It involves words that are rich in meaning including conversational, general academic, and domain-specific words. Oral vocabulary is the set of words which students learn through listening to various media, to text read aloud, and through conversations. Emergent readers have a much larger oral vocabulary than print vocabulary. Developing students' oral vocabulary will help them to better comprehend text read aloud to them. Oral vocabulary also helps readers recognize and make sense of words they see in print.

Comprehension of complex text depends on understanding the words in a selection, and competent writing requires extensive and specific word knowledge. Students learn the meanings of many words indirectly as they listen to spoken language. As they read, they build rich and flexible word knowledge through informal talk, discussion, reading literature and informational texts independently, and by listening to text read aloud.

The words that have the most impact on students' reading achievement are academic, or Tier 2, words. These words appear in a lot of texts and are the ones that students are least likely to know.

Tier 1 words are those commonly used in speech, such as *mom, table,* and *book.* Little instructional time needs to spent on these words, unless the student is an English learner.

Tier 2 words are those words found in many sources and have wide applicability, such as *compare, enormous,* and *vital.* A lack of knowledge of these words can severely hinder comprehension of text. A significant amount of instructional time should focus on these words.

Tier 3 words are those content-specific domain words that relate to science, history, social studies, or math. Domain words, such as *lava, adaptation, bipartisan,* and *Louisiana Purchase,* do not appear in many sources and can be taught at point of use.

> ❝ Becoming literate depends on the fast, accurate recognition of words in texts so that readers can focus their attention on meaning. ❞
>
> – Dr. Donald Bear

Research

- Vocabulary development is linked to reading comprehension. Students need multiple exposures to new words to master them, and both indirect and direct vocabulary instruction are key to this mastery.

- Words must be taught in context of the texts students are reading and not from random lists of vocabulary words. Meaning is derived from the phrases and sentences before and after the new vocabulary word. Instruction must be supported by many examples of vocabulary words in context. (*Wonders* program author Donald Bear)

- Morphological knowledge is related to word knowledge and reading comprehension (Nagy, Berninger, & Abbott, 2006, Nagy, 2007).

- Morphological knowledge of academic words may be particularly important for academic achievement, given the morphological complexity of many academic words (Corson, 1997), and the Greek or Latin origins of 82% of the words in the Academic Word List (Coxhead, 2000).

How Does *Wonders* Teach Vocabulary?

The vocabulary lessons in *Wonders* focus on high-frequency words for early elementary students and include direct instruction on low-frequency words to support all students on the path to acquiring reading strength. Students at all grade levels have multiple encounters with new words. In Grades K and 1 there is direct instruction of oral vocabulary, while at Grades 2—5 there are direct instructional vocabulary minilessons.

In Grades 2—5, each genre study provides many opportunities for students to learn and practice using new vocabulary.

- **Vocabulary Minilessons** The Words in Context section of each minilesson introduces students to academic vocabulary that will help them understand and discuss the concept they will learn and read about. These vocabulary words appear in texts throughout the genre study giving students multiple exposures to the words in context. Each lesson focuses on a key **Vocabulary Strategy** students will study throughout the year. These include: Context Clues; Prefixes, Suffixes, and Root Words; Use Print or Digital Resources; Idioms, Synonyms, Antonyms, Homophones, and Homographs.

- **Vocabulary Cards** These cards are digital resources you can print out and use to reinforce word meanings.

- **Build Vocabulary** As students read the Anchor Text, you can use the words and definitions provided in this feature to help students learn more vocabulary words in context, including domain-specific words.

- **Academic Language** In each lesson, *Wonders* identifies high-utility instructional words that can be used by students across academic disciplines. Where applicable, Spanish-language cognates are listed.

- **Spiral Review** Repeated exposures are critical to learning new vocabulary. Vocabulary words from other genre studies are reviewed during each genre study.

- **ELL Vocabulary** The routine on ELL Visual Vocabulary Cards can be used to preteach additional words from the Shared Read and Leveled Reader.

- **High-Frequency Words** At the beginning of the year, all students will review high-frequency words. Throughout the year, a systematic review of approximately 250 of the most common words is offered for Approaching Level students.

What Does Success Look Like?

Observe students during the Guided Practice sections of their Vocabulary lessons and while participating in the Expand Vocabulary activities. Assess students' individual word building work on a weekly basis for both required and optional assignments, including finding interesting words and their meanings, creating word webs, synonym lists, and other word study activities. Students should be able to apply the various vocabulary strategies taught in the lessons and activities to determine the meaning of unfamiliar words. They should be proficient at using vocabulary strategies such as context and sentence clues to unlock word meaning. Students should be comfortable utilizing a variety of approaches to derive word meaning, including how to use compound words, multiple meaning words, prefixes and suffixes, similes, root words, homophones, Greek and Latin roots, idioms, synonyms, and metaphors to deepen their understanding and enrich their reading.

> 66 It is impossible to teach students all the words they need to know. Rather, the goal is to teach students how to examine and think about words. 99
>
> – Dr. Donald Bear

Routines

The routine in this section aligns with the lessons provided in the **Teacher's Edition,** but allows you to take a flexible approach to teaching vocabulary so you can meet the needs of all your students.

Vocabulary Routines

- Vocabulary
- Define/Explain/Ask

Vocabulary Routine

1. **Introduce** Explain to students they will learn about new words.

   Today we will learn new vocabulary words. I will say a vocabulary word, define it, and use it in a sentence. Then, I will ask you to use the word in a sentence. The more we practice using the new words, the better readers and writers we will be.

2. **Model (I Do)** Model the task by introducing and using several new vocabulary words. Use the Define/Explain/Ask Routine.

   I am going to say the vocabulary word so you can hear the correct pronunciation. Then I am going to define it, use it in a sentence, and ask you a question about it.

3. **Guided Practice (We Do)** Throughout the week, provide daily opportunities for students to use and apply the words. Daily activities are included in the Teacher's Edition. These include sentence starters, exploring different forms of the words, and other vocabulary-building strategies developed by Beck and McKeown.

   I am going to describe some things. If what I describe is an example of people cooperating, say cooperate. *If it is not, do not say anything.*

   - *Two children setting the table for dinner*
   - *Two children grabbing the same book*
   - *Two children putting crayons back in the box*

   After you have introduced several words, provide additional opportunities to apply and differentiate between new words.

4. **Independent Practice (You Do)** Individual turns allow you an opportunity to assess each student's skill level and provide additional practice for those students who need it.

   Near the end of each week, students should write sentences in their word study notebooks using the words.

> **Teaching Tip**
>
> Introduce vocabulary words before students read the selection or while reading the text aloud. If you read aloud, pause to give a brief explanation for each word you have chosen to teach. Teach the words after reading the story.

Define/Example/Ask Vocabulary Routine

Use the Visual Vocabulary Cards to introduce new vocabulary words. Follow the instructions on the back of the card. For example,

1. **Define:** Define the word in simple, student-friendly language.

   To cooperate is to work together to get something done.

2. **Example:** Provide an example of how the word in a meaningful sentence, relevant to students' lives.

   I cooperate with my sister to clean our room.

3. **Ask:** Ask questions that require students to apply the word. They can give an example or explanation, or identify a synonym or antonym.

   How do you and your family cooperate to get jobs done?

Additional Strategies for Teaching Vocabulary

Choosing Words for Instruction *Wonders* focuses on instructing those words that have the most impact on students' reading achievement, which are the academic, or Tier 2, words. These words appear in a lot of texts and are the ones that students are least likely to know. Tier 1 words are those commonly used in speech, such as *mom, table,* and *book.* Little instructional time needs to be spent on these words, unless the student is an English learner. Tier 2 words are those words found in many sources and have wide applicability, such as *compare, enormous,* and *vital.* A lack of knowledge of these words can severely hinder comprehension of text. A significant amount of instructional time should focus on these words. Tier 3 words are those content-specific domain words that relate to science, history, social studies, or math. Domain words, such as *lava, adaptation, bipartisan,* and *Louisiana Purchase*, do not appear in many sources and can be taught at point of use.

Building Oral Vocabulary Use Big Books and Interactive Read-Alouds to teach new vocabulary words. Teach vocabulary words from the selections including Tier 2 words, academic vocabulary, domain words, or other unfamiliar words. Use "Talk About It" Weekly Openers to develop oral vocabulary and help build background knowledge for the concept of the week, and to aid in students' comprehension of texts read throughout the week. Use the words generated by discussion of the photograph as a way of introducing selected oral vocabulary.

Make the Most of the Build Your Word List During every Shared Read vocabulary lesson students are directed to find interesting and important words. Students keep track of their vocabulary words in a dedicated vocabulary or writing notebook. Students can follow the directions given in each Build Your Word List activity to deepen their knowledge of the word. In addition, students can follow this routine:

1. Collect the word. Find an important, interesting, or difficult word. Read around the word and think about its possible meaning.

2. Record the word and sentence. Sometimes sentences are too long, so parts of the sentence can be recorded.

3. "Take apart." Separate word parts—prefixes, suffixes, roots, and bases.

4. Think of related words. Brainstorm related words by word parts—prefixes, suffixes, roots, and bases.

5. Study the word in the dictionary and other resources, and record related words and interesting information.

6. Review and share. Prepare an explanation for each word part to share with classmates.

Word Squares Ask students to create Word Squares for each word in their word study notebooks.

- In the first square, students write the word.
- In the second square, students write their own definitions of the word and any related words, such as synonyms. Remind students that synonyms are words that mean the same or nearly the same. Related words include words with the same base, such as succeed, success, successful; adapt, adaptation.
- In the third square, students draw a simple illustration that will help them remember the word. They might also want to write a mnemonic that will help them remember the word. (example: A mentor helps me learn.)
- In the fourth square, students write nonexamples, including antonyms for the word. Remind students that antonyms are words that mean the opposite. (example: succeed/fail)

Word Square

Succeed	achieve goal win success successful
	fall failure disappointment

Teaching Academic Vocabulary These five principals of academic vocabulary study can guide instruction and expand students' thinking about word meanings.

1. **Vocabulary is linked to concept development.**

   Words describe ideas, and, in discussions of vocabulary, students expand and refine their thinking. The key to vocabulary learning is to uncover the concepts that underlie the vocabulary.

2. **Vocabulary is learned in context.**

   Students learn new vocabulary from their reading and writing. Teaching students the strategies to unlock meaning of unfamiliar words is crucial to acquiring new vocabulary.

3. **Vocabulary is not about teaching just words.**

   To learn new words, students need to look at words in context, to examine the words in the sentences and phrases that come before and after the word.

4. **Vocabulary instruction is deep and generative.**

   "When students learn one word, the learn ten words." Studying related words and phrases expands the knowledge of the underlying words.

5. **Vocabulary instruction involves the study of morphology, the structure of words.**

   Learning the meaning of prefixes and suffixes make it possible for students to derive the meaning of base words and roots.

READING

Foster a Love of Reading

Literacy begins with firm foundations. But learning to read is so much more. Students must combine what they already know with the new skills and strategies they are acquiring. They must learn to figure out what text says, how it says it, and what it means. They must be able to summarize, cite text evidence to answer text dependent questions, and think metacognitively, as well as talk about and respond in writing as they read.

Because literacy unlocks all other learning, we want students to become self-directed, critical readers. Academic success is linked to reading determination and perseverance. Each piece of the *Wonders* reading puzzle supports what we believe to be true.

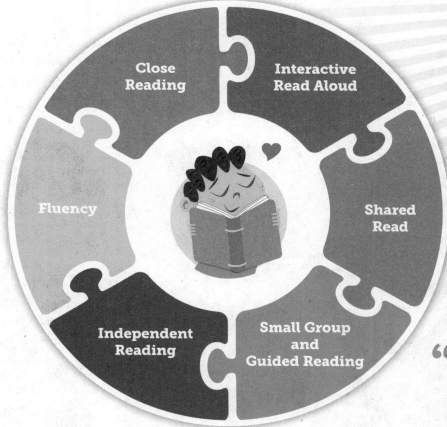

Close Reading

Interactive Read Aloud

Shared Read

Small Group and Guided Reading

Independent Reading

Fluency

seamuss/Shutterstock

> **The right approach, at the right time, for the right type of learning.**
> – Dr. Douglas Fisher

Wonders gives you the tools to equip your students with the skills and strategies they need to become confident readers.

- During **Close Reading**, students read widely across connected texts. They take notes, participate in collaborative conversations while using text evidence to support their ideas, and respond to prompts by writing analytically.

- **Interactive Read Alouds** introduce the genre and comprehension strategy to your students.

- To equip all students with the tools they need to unlock complex text, the **Shared Reads** provide multiple opportunities for teaching, modeling, guided practice, and practice.

- You know what your students need, and we have the resources to help. **Small Groups** and **Guided Reading** lessons help you meet your students where they are and help them become stronger, more confident readers.

- When students engage in **Independent Reading** it helps them learn to apply information in new ways and develop the confidence to read and reflect on texts as self-directed, critical thinkers.

- **Fluency** is important because students who read fluently can focus on comprehension and new vocabulary.

wavebreakmedia/Shutterstock

Close Reading

What You Need to Know About Close Reading

Close reading is an approach to teaching students how to become self-directed readers. When students close read, they actively engage with complex texts and use strategies to think critically about and dig deeply into texts. They learn to take notes, ask questions, and understand their purpose for reading. That's important because as your students think about, analyze, and make decisions as they read, they gain literary and cultural knowledge while developing a deep understanding of various text structures and elements.

Close reading helps your students become better readers in all content areas as they progress through the grades.

Research

- Studies show that instructional procedures that encourage students to pay especially close attention to what a text says have positive impacts on reading comprehension. Researchers found that careful summarization of text improves reading comprehension especially during the elementary grades (Graham & Hebert, 2010; NICHD, 2000).

- Text-dependent questions are used in reading instruction to promote the habit of rereading text in order to build schema (Fisher & Frey, in press; Pearson & Johnson, 1978). These questions are designed to cause students to return to the text. This is important when text is being used to build knowledge.

- Research shows that comprehension skills and strategies, in isolation, are not sufficient for fostering students' comprehension skills. Students must learn to apply these skills to complex text (*Reading Between the Lines*, ACT Inc., 2006).

> **Students read easier books on the same topic or easier versions of the challenging text in bite-sized chunks, rather than all at once. It is sort of like climbing stairs: each step brings you closer to the level that you are reaching for.**
>
> — Dr. Timothy Shanahan

FatCamera/E+/Getty Images

How Does *Wonders* Teach Close Reading?

In *Wonders*, students learn to close read by carefully examining a variety of engaging and complex texts. In this chart, you can see how *Wonders'* components are used to teach, model, and help students practice close reading.

Did You Know?

Anchor Charts Program author Kathy Bumgardner calls anchor charts "learning velcro" for your teaching. They are valuable resources for your students to refer to as they encounter other texts and learning scenarios. Create anchor charts with your students to help them remember characteristics of genres and comprehension strategies.

Introduce the Genre	Introduce the genre and comprehension strategy using the **Interactive Read Aloud**. Help students create anchor charts and use Think Alouds to model the strategy.
Teach the Shared Read	Read the **Shared Read**. Focus on the Read prompts to teach and model close reading. Use the mini lessons and Access Complex Text (ACT) scaffolds as needed.
Teach Craft and Structure	Reread small sections of the Shared Read. Students talk about and cite text evidence to answer text dependent questions. Focus on the Reread prompts here.
Respond to Reading	Use the writing prompt to help students use their notes, analyze text evidence, and respond to what they read. The sentence starters help focus discussion. For the Response Routine, see page 90.
Read the Anchor Text	Apply the Close Reading Routine as students read the **Anchor Text**. Use the Read and Reread prompts, Access Complex Text boxes, and metacognitive prompts in your **Teacher's Edition** to guide practice and help students practice close reading on their own. Students can respond to the Reread prompts, and then use their notes to write an analytical short response to what they read.
Make Connections	After reading and rereading the **Paired Selection**, your students respond to the Reread prompts and then make connections using the **Integrate** prompt.
Teach in Small Groups	Teach in small groups using the **Leveled Reader** lessons to support all students and accelerate progress. **Differentiated Genre Passages** are one more way students can practice skills and strategies and make connections using a text targeted to their proficiency level.
Encourage Independent Reading	Students can choose books for 30–40 minutes of daily independent reading and respond in their writer's notebooks. Use the **Classroom Library** Trade books and bonus Leveled Readers—both with lessons available online—to encourage independent reading. There are also online **Unit Bibliographies** to help students self-select independent reading texts.

Check This Out!

There are two Classroom Library books per unit per grade. And for each trade book, there is an 8-page lesson, including four pages for your students to practice close reading.

A Word About Complex Text

Complex text is high-quality text that includes a wide range of literature from different cultures and time periods. It includes informational text that will help students build a foundation of knowledge in science, social studies, and math. This is important because it provides the opportunity for meaningful close reading. There are three factors to consider when determining the complexity of a text:

Quantitative Measures are "countable" features that can be calculated by a computer. The Lexile Framework for Reading uses word frequency and sentence length to measure text complexity. Lexile scores of all *Wonders* texts are clearly identified and progress within and among grades.

Qualitative Measures use specific features of how a text is written or the topic of a text to determine what makes it complex. In *Wonders*, Access Complex Text boxes provide scaffolded instruction, teaching suggestions, and prompts for seven different elements that may make a text complex:

- Purpose
- Organization
- Connection of Ideas
- Sentence Structure
- Genre
- Specific Vocabulary
- Prior Knowledge

Reader/Task Considerations The readers' engagement, knowledge of concept, and interest influence complexity of a text, as well as the questions and tasks applied to it.

What Does Success Look Like?

As you walk around your classroom, observe your students as they work alone, in pairs, or in small groups during guided practice and independent practice times. You should see and hear students

- rereading small passages of text to answer text-dependent questions;
- asking and answering questions as they read;
- annotating texts and identifying key ideas and details;
- actively engaging in collaborative conversations where they are sharing their opinions and ideas and using text evidence to support their thoughts and opinions;
- using text evidence to respond in writing to deeper level questions.

Routines

The routines in this section align with the lessons provided in the **Teacher's Edition** but allow you to take a flexible approach to teaching close reading to meet the needs of all your students.

Close Reading Routines

- Close Reading
- Finding Text Evidence
- Minilesson
- Respond to the Text
- Retelling

Close Reading Routine

Teaching Tip

Access Complex Text Use the ACT prompts during the Read step when the complexity of the text features makes it hard for students to understand the selection.

1. **READ** The purpose of the first read is to figure out what the selection is about. Students read the text through to identify key ideas and details, take notes, and summarize. Depending upon the needs of your students, you can

   - ask students to read the text silently;
   - read the text together with students;
   - read the text aloud.

   Model how to take notes, find text evidence, and answer text-dependent questions. At the end of the first read, help students summarize the selection.

Corrective Feedback

Observe students to be sure they are going back into the text to reread small chunks as they look for text evidence to answer questions. Provide feedback on text evidence they cite and the conclusions they make. Allow students to provide feedback to each other as well.

2. **REREAD** With students, reread short chunks of the text to answer deeper level questions about craft and structure. Have them reread to

   - analyze words and phrases the author uses and how these words and phrases affect the text's meaning;
   - work together to find and cite text evidence to text-dependent questions;
   - use the **Reading/Writing Companion** to discuss, cite text evidence, and write short responses to text-dependent questions.

3. **INTEGRATE** In the Integrate phase, students go back into the texts to critically evaluate and compare them. The goal is to help students make deeper connections within the texts and between texts. Have students use the Reading/Writing Companion to

   - talk about and compare the selections they read with a photograph, song, poem, painting, mural, or sketch;
   - be inspired to act.

Finding Text Evidence Routine

1. **Explain** Briefly explain the routine and its purpose.

   Text evidence are the words and illustrations in a text that support an answer to a question, argument, or conclusion you make about that text.

2. **Model** Ask students a text-dependent question and model how to locate text evidence.

   I am going to go back into the text. I will reread to find relevant or important words, phrases, or sentences that support my answer. I might find text that states the answer to the question. I might find text that helps me figure out or make an inference to determine the answer. I will use the text evidence to state or write the answer to the question in my own words.

3. **Guided Practice** Pose other text-dependent questions. Work together with students to find text evidence to answer the questions. Encourage students to generate their own questions. The Your Turn prompts in the **Reading/Writing Companion** provide guided practice for finding text evidence to questions.

4. **Practice** Have students work independently or in small groups to identify and cite text evidence. The Your Turn prompts may be used for practice. As students work independently or with a partner, walk around the classroom and monitor students' progress as they work. Offer support and corrective feedback as needed.

Corrective Feedback

If students cite strong evidence, discuss why it is strong. If students cite parts of the text that are not relevant or not strong, reread with students the more appropriate text evidence. Explain why it helps support the answer. Then have students restate their answer using the text evidence.

Minilesson Routine

1. **Explain** Define the skill and its purpose for students. Create or add to Anchor Charts to help students remember characteristics of the text's genre and comprehension skills and strategies.

2. **Model** Reread the text and model how to apply the skill or strategy to the text.

3. **Guided Practice** Ask a question and work with students to answer it. Then have them use the Your Turn prompt to practice with a partner.

4. **Practice** Have students work independently or with partner to complete the Your Turn prompts.

Respond to the Text Routine

This response routine helps students to answer rigorous questions about the text.

Corrective Feedback

If students need support talking about the text or finding text evidence, use Think Alouds to model how to use the sentence starters to focus discussion and find evidence in the text.

1. **Talk** Read the question prompts in the **Reading/Writing Companion** with students. Have them work with a partner to discuss the text.

   Turn to a partner and talk about the question. Go back and reread a section of the text and find evidence to support your thoughts and ideas. Use the sentence starters to help you focus your discussion.

2. **Cite** Use the graphic organizer to record text evidence to answer the question. Remind students to record details that answer the question.

3. **Write** Have students write a response to the question using the notes they took in the graphic organizer.

Retelling Routine

Retelling allows you to monitor comprehension. Use this routine as you guide children to retell.

1. **Model Retelling** After finishing a passage or selection, use a Think Aloud to model retelling. Use the text or an illustration and retell in your own words.

   Think Aloud I read on this page that Little Flap was scared and didn't want to tell his friends. He acted bravely by flapping his wings. He wanted Tuff and Fluff to see that he wasn't afraid. But I can see in the illustration how scared Little Flap is.

2. **Guide Retelling** Encourage children to use the important features, such as key details in the illustrations or in the text, to help them to remember what the text is about.

   When we retell, we use our own words to tell what the selection is about. We can find clues in the text or illustrations to help us retell.

3. **Discuss the Retelling** Have children summarize selection concepts by asking them higher-order questions. Refer to the Professional Development video for more instruction.

Teaching Tip

When applicable, use the words *beginning, middle,* and *end* to help guide students in their retelling.

Additional Strategies for Teaching Close Reading

More Scaffolding For students who need the extra support of a scaffolded lesson, use a Think Aloud to model how to annotate and take notes using a small chunk of text. Ask students a text-dependent question and help them identify and organize evidence to form a written response.

Picture Clues Authors and illustrators work together to create texts that are meaningful and complex. Try using a book without words and ask students questions that require them to find clues and evidence in illustrations and photographs.

Super Summarizers Help students practice summarizing by asking them to:

- write a one-act play depicting a section of text.
- create a book jacket. Have students choose a section or chapter and draw an illustration for the front of the front of the book jacket. Then ask them to write a short summary for the back cover.
- create a movie poster depicting one chapter or section of the selection they are reading.

Ask More Questions! Encourage students to ask and answer questions before they read, as they read, and after they read. Create a class chart and ask students to record their questions on one side. Then have students cite text evidence to answer them. Ask students to write their responses and evidence on the chart.

Annotation Station Set up a workstation with highlighters, colored pencils, markers, and sticky notes. Encourage students to use the fun supplies to annotate as they read. At the station, place a chart showing different ways students can annotate text as they close read.

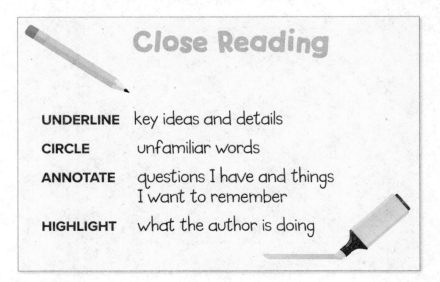

Close Reading

UNDERLINE	key ideas and details
CIRCLE	unfamiliar words
ANNOTATE	questions I have and things I want to remember
HIGHLIGHT	what the author is doing

Favorite Author Study Find books by the same author and have students work independently or in small groups to compare and contrast what the author does to make each text interesting. Ask them to create a chart or poster noting things like text features, organization, and word choice for informational texts; and characters and setting, illustrations, and figurative language for fiction.

Patterns As students reread chunks of text, have them look for patterns. Ask them what the author does consistently to help them better understand a topic. For example:

- Does the author use definitions to help you understand unfamiliar words?
- What does the author do to help you picture in your mind what the characters are thinking?
- How does the author use text features?

Games, Activities, and More Have students use the Differentiated Workstation Cards independently or in small groups. They can also use the interactive reading games and activities on **my.mheducation.com.**

A Few Words About Depth of Knowledge and Close Reading

In *Wonders*, the phases of Close Reading are aligned with Webb's Depth of Knowledge (DOK) model.

- **DOK 1** questions focus on recall and ask students to define, label, tell, recognize, quote, use, and state.

- **DOK 2** questions require students to classify, compare, predict, infer, summarize, make observations, and show.

- **DOK 3** questions focus on strategic thinking, such as revising, formulating, drawing conclusions, and assessing.

- **DOK 4** questions extend thinking, and include synthesizing information, applying concepts, analyzing, creating, and making connections.

Interactive Read Aloud

What You Need to Know About Interactive Read Alouds

A read aloud is a planned oral reading of a text. It gives your students the chance to hear you model and demonstrate the strategies that are used by proficient readers. When you gather your students and read aloud, you are showing them what fluent reading looks and sounds like. Using interactive read alouds in your daily instruction provides students with purposeful opportunities to think deeply and talk about texts. It also helps your students understand that there are many different ways of getting information.

Research

- Research shows that read alouds engage students, help them develop background knowledge, increase comprehension skills, and support language development (Beck and McKeown, 2001).

- Studies have also found that children who are read to on a daily basis develop the motivation and love of reading that is critical to their reading success (Cunningham, 2005).

How Does *Wonders* Teach Interactive Read Alouds?

Within each week or genre study, you will find a variety of texts to use in lessons that deepen your students' knowledge of a particular genre, beginning with the Interactive Read Aloud. The Interactive Read Aloud introduces the genre and reading strategy. In *Wonders*, use the **Interactive Read Alouds** to:

- connect to the concept by talking with students about the Essential Question.
- preview the genre, talk about the features of the genre, and create an anchor chart.
- preview the comprehension strategy and use Think Alouds to model it. *Wonders* focuses on the following specific, effective, and research-based strategies:
    - Making Predictions
    - Visualizing
    - Summarizing
    - Rereading
    - Asking and Answering Questions
- read the text and model the strategy, and talk about vocabulary.
- reinforce how you use the strategy with Think Aloud Clouds. These serve as visual cues to help students remember and apply reading strategies.
- have students retell or summarize the selection.

The Interactive Read Aloud lessons in your **Teacher's Edition** gives you the tools to help you carry out explicit and formal instruction in the strategies students need to get a leg up on reading comprehension. There are also additional images related to the Read Alouds online at **my.mheducation.com** that encourage audio-visual connections and group discussion.

> **Did You Know?**
>
> When you model reading strategies using interactive read alouds and Think Alouds—and explain why you are modeling them—you help your students understand how to problem solve and comprehend what they are reading.

Think Aloud Card

IRA Cards

> 66 **Focusing on genre teaches students to use the appropriate strategies to unlock a text.** 99
>
> – Dr. Timonthy Shanahan

What If I Want To Choose My Own Read Alouds?

Wonders has Interactive Read Alouds with support in both print and online. But if you want to choose your own texts to use with your students, here are some guidelines.

Effective read alouds require a lot of careful planning. Below is a framework for developing strong read aloud lessons using rich, authentic texts.

Prepare Decide on when you will use strategic read alouds in your daily instruction. Choose anywhere from 1–4 times a day to read aloud to your students. Choose

- one longer read (10–15 minutes) to build comprehension and stamina; the others can be "quick reads" (1–3 minutes) that you squeeze in throughout the day;
- high-quality and high-interest texts that will engage students, provide opportunities for thinking deeply, and include a variety of texts. Think carefully about the purpose of each text. Also, be sure the text is appropriate for all students in your class. Be sensitive to the range of cultures and personality types, and steer away from controversial or upsetting topics.

Read and reread the selection to determine what part of the text you will read aloud.

Develop your reading goals Be clear about what the purpose is for reading the text and what the goals are.

Analyze the text to help students Access Complex Text by determining the characteristics of a specific text that make it challenging. See page 87 for more information about ACT.

Practice reading the text aloud Get comfortable reading it with appropriate expression and tone. Rehearse unfamiliar names and invented words so that you can pronounce them correctly and without error. Time your reading to make certain the text works with your allotted time frame for the read aloud.

Read Gather students together in a circle around you or in a group on the rug, making sure everyone can see the book.

- Preview and explore vocabulary, if necessary. Talk about the genre, introduce the book, and explain why you chose it. Point out the title and cover illustration and ask students to think of questions before they read.
- Read the text fluently, pausing to ask questions. Read with animation and expression, as applicable. Vary the pace of your reading, use plenty of eye contact, and include dramatic pauses when appropriate.

AVAVA/Shutterstock

- Model strategies using Think Alouds.
- Ask text-dependent questions. Help students use text evidence and picture clues to support their answers.
- Pause to give your students the chance to interact. Engage them in discussion that focuses both on their comprehension of the text and their engagement with the text. Have students make connections between the text and their own lives.

Respond Discuss the element of the read aloud with your students. Ask them to think about other text you have read or they have read independently that were the same genre. Then have student briefly retell or summarize the text in their own words.

What Does Success Look Like?

As you read aloud to your students, they should be

- listening attentively;
- interacting and participating when asked;
- turning and talking with a partner when prompted;
- actively engaged in collaborative conversations and sharing their opinions and ideas;
- using text evidence to support their ideas and thoughts;
- using key details to summarize or retell the read aloud.

FatCamera/E+/Getty Images

Routines

The routines in this section align with the lessons provided in the **Teacher's Edition**, but allow you to take a flexible approach to using Interactive Read Alouds to meet the needs of all students.

Interactive Read Aloud Routines

- Interactive Read Aloud Cards
- Retelling

Interactive Read Aloud Cards Routine

1. Display and point out key elements in the illustrations or photographs as you read the text.

2. Introduce highlighted words using the **Define/Example/Ask** routine on page 78. You may wish to read the selection once and then go back and use the routine with the highlighted words.

3. Use the collaborative conversations prompts to encourage students to use the new vocabulary with their partners.

4. Use the Retell suggestions to guide students in retelling the selection.

Retelling Routine

1. Introduce students to retelling by displaying the Interactive Read Aloud cards.

2. Use the Retell questions to guide children to recall the basic events and contents of the text.

3. When applicable, use the words *beginning, middle,* and *end* to help guide students' retelling.

4. Ask higher-level questions that prompt students to summarize story concepts.

Corrective Feedback

If students are using vocabulary words correctly, point out how they are using the words. If students are unable to use the vocabulary words, go back and reread sections of the text to help them figure out the meaning of the words.

Additional Strategies for Teaching Interactive Read Alouds

Invite Engagement There are many ways you can encourage your students to engage with the text. Some ideas include: encouraging them to find letters or words they know; chime in and read phrases aloud with you; or clap their hands when they hear a special word.

Act Out Use gestures as you read. Then reread and have students mimic the gestures you make. Have partners work together to replay one section of the text.

Make Predictions As you read, pause and ask students to turn to a partner and predict what will happen next. Then read on, pause again, and have students confirm or revise their prediction.

Extend Vocabulary Model how to use a vocabulary word in a new oral sentence. Act out the sentence as you say it. Invite students to make up their own sentences they can say and act out to show the vocabulary word.

Word Sort Have children write vocabulary words on cards. Then have partners sort the cards into categories. For example, words that name an action, words that describe, or words that name a thing.

Compare and Contrast When you finish a group of read alouds on the same topic, have students work in small groups on a chart showing how they are the same and how they are different. Students can also make connections across texts.

Summary Poster Instead of having students summarize the text, ask them to create a poster showing what the selection was about. Have them note at least three important details in their poster. Ask students to share their posters with a partner.

Take a Snapshot Ask students to think of one key idea from the read aloud and illustrate it. Tell them they will be creating a snapshot of the main idea from a section of the read aloud they choose. Have students share their snapshots by telling about it in one sentence.

Shared Read

What You Need to Know About Shared Reads

The Shared Read has it all. It is a complex text that can hold up to analysis. It is challenging, yet short. It lends itself to annotation or "reading with a pencil." Using a Shared Read to teach and model close reading will give your students the opportunity to not only practice new skills, but also to also to reread, respond to questions that guide their thinking, and interact with others about the content.

It's no secret that when students learn to close read, they not only develop a deep understanding of texts, but they also learn how to think critically, integrate new knowledge, and dig deeper into increasingly complex texts. As you and your students read and reread the Shared Read for different purposes, they learn to annotate, ask and answer questions about what they are reading, talk about, cite text evidence, and apply what they are learning about genre, comprehension, vocabulary, and writing.

Research

- Research shows that teaching a variety of reading comprehension strategies leads to increased learning of the strategies, to specific transfer of learning, to increased memory and understanding of new passages, and, in some cases, to general improvements in comprehension (NICHHD, 2000, p. 4–52).

- The National Reading Panel identified seven strategies as having "a firm scientific basis for concluding that they improve comprehension in normal readers" (NICHHD, 2000, p. 4–42)—demonstrating that comprehension can be improved through explicit, formal instruction in such strategies. And, the U.S. Department of Education's What Works Clearinghouse verified that several of these strategies were effective, even in the primary grades (Shanahan, et al., 2010).

> **" Using appropriate complex texts and providing instruction and modeling on the strategies to access complex texts enable students to become proficient independent readers of a wide range of text of increasing complexity, including a wide range of genre and topics. "**
>
> — Kathy Bumgardner

How Does *Wonders* Teach with the Shared Read?

In *Wonders*, each week or genre study contains a Shared Read related to the Essential Question. The Shared Read appears in the **Reading/Writing Companion** with prompts that guide students through the Read and Reread steps of the Close Reading Routine.

The Shared Read can be used flexibly, working with every stage of the gradual release of responsibility model. Depending on your students' needs, you can use it to provide focused instruction, guided instruction, collaborative learning, and independent learning as students read and reread the text. You can read the text with the whole class or a small group, using prompts to teach and model reading strategies. You may choose to have some students read and respond to the prompts independently or with a partner before discussing with a small group or the whole class. You may also choose to preteach some vocabulary for some or all of your students. You'll find suggestions for differentiating instruction in your **Teacher's Edition** on the first page of each Shared Read.

Each Shared Read has companion mini-lessons that focus on a vocabulary strategy, a comprehension skill and strategy, genre, and literary elements or text features. One Shared Read in each unit provides an opportunity for building fluency by having students reread portions of the text with a partner.

What Does Success Look Like?

- Students interact with the text, annotating and taking notes as they read.
- Students cite text evidence when responding to prompts.
- Students can summarize the text after their first read.
- Students reread text to clarify information, find text evidence, and analyze author's craft.
- Students participate in collaborative conversations about text, supporting each other as they explore challenging vocabulary and interesting word choice; apply reading skills and strategies; and build knowledge about genre, text features, and literary elements.

Routines

The Shared Read routine in this section aligns with the lessons provided in the **Teacher's Edition**, but it allows you to take a flexible approach so you can meet the needs of all your students.

Shared Read Routine

1. **Set a purpose.** Before students read the Shared Read, have them preview the text and think about the genre study's Essential Question. Then have them set a purpose for reading by responding to the prompt in the **Reading/Writing Companion.** Remind them to annotate the text as they read, noting interesting words and key details.

2. **Read the text.** Students read the text through once to get the gist of the selection.

3. **Respond to Read prompts.** Guide students to answer the prompts in the Reading/Writing Companion. Provide modeling and/or scaffolding as needed. The **Teacher's Edition** offers support for the prompts in the Reading/Writing Companion and provides additional prompts with scaffolding for students who need extra guidance.

4. **Summarize.** Have students use their notes to orally summarize the text with a partner. Then have them write a summary in their writer's notebook.

5. **Respond to Reread prompts.** Guide students to answer the Reread prompts collaboratively to analyze the author's craft and text structure. Encourage students to reread the text during this process. The Teacher's Edition offers scaffolding suggestions for these prompts on the Craft and Structure pages.

Additional Strategies for Teaching with the Shared Read

Summary Strategy Guide students to use the Somebody-Wanted-But-So strategy (Macon, Bewell, & Vogt, 1991) to summarize stories. This simple framework focuses students on the main character(s), the problem, the actions taken to resolve the problem, and the resolution, helping them identify the key elements of a narrative instead of retelling every detail.

Graphic Organizers Give students a graphic organizer to organize and focus their summary. Graphic organizers for narrative and informational texts are available at **my.mheducation.com**.

Super Summaries Offer students options for creating and presenting their summaries. They may choose to act the summary out, record it digitally, or illustrate it in a series of comic strip panels.

Build Fluency Pairs can practice and then record themselves reading dialogue fluently with the Audio Recorder.

Gagliardilmages/Shutterstock

Small Group and Guided Reading

What You Need to Know About Small Group and Guided Reading

> **Changing the size of the group I'm going to teach is something that I do strategically. I teach individuals or smaller groups or the whole class based on what I'm trying to accomplish.**
>
> – Dr. Timothy Shanahan

One of the most difficult challenges you face as teachers is how to deal with the multiple levels and learning needs of your students. Small group reading is an approach in which a teacher works with a small group of students who have similar instructional needs. Some small groups are formed around the strategy needs of students. In guided reading, groups are formed based on students' similar guided reading levels. The goal of all small group reading is to provide targeted, differentiated teaching to support every student's reading development.

Ideally, small groups should include no more than six students, but may have as many as eight. Student observations and formative assessments are used to determine membership for strategy groups. For guided reading groups, running records are used to determine a student's guided reading level. In most small groups, the members of the group read the same text—one that is accessible enough for them to understand, but also includes opportunities for problem solving as students apply reading strategies. Group membership is dynamic; groups will change as students' needs and reading levels change.

At the start of each small group lesson, teachers provide some background information on the text and state the purpose of the lesson. Then, students read quietly or silently to themselves. As they read, the teacher confers with individual students, leaning in to listen and prompt strategy use. At the end of each lesson, students discuss their understanding of the text and may share examples of how they used strategies as they read. Keep in mind that small group instruction is a tool that should be used strategically, for a clear purpose.

Research

- Teaching students in whole and small groups has proven more effective for student achievement gains than teaching solely in whole groups (Tilly 2003; Vaughn 2003).

How Does *Wonders* Teach Small Group and Guided Reading?

Wonders includes whole group Shared Read lessons that you can use to model and explain skills and strategies. Then, with your support, students practice and apply those skills to the Anchor Text. Based on Check for Success observations of students and assessment information from the Data Dashboard, you may decide that some students would benefit from small group instruction. The *Wonders* **Teacher's Edition** provides Differentiated Instruction small group lessons on vocabulary and comprehension at four different levels: Approaching, On Level, Beyond Level, and English Language Learners. Phonics/decoding and fluency lessons are also provided for the Approaching Level.

Each genre study is also accompanied by topic-related Leveled Readers and Genre Passages for small group instruction at four different levels (Approaching, On Level, Beyond Level, and ELL), as well as instructional support for them in the Teacher's Edition.

You can search the Leveled Reader Database at **my.mheducation.com** for more leveled titles to use as you teach small groups. The database is searchable by Theme, Keyword, Genre, Skill, Text Feature, Grade Range, Lexile, and Guided Reading Level.

The *Assessment Handbook* and the Data Dashboard at **my.mheducation.com** provide more information on assessments you can use to form small groups. The *Running Records/Benchmark Books* resource provides leveled passages and recording forms for determining students' guided reading levels.

What Does Success Look Like?

As you listen to students reading during a small group lesson, look for their ability to apply the strategy you are focusing on. During student discussions at the end of a small group reading lessons, be sure students' contributions show that they have comprehended the text.

McGraw-Hill Education/Ken Karp

Routines

The routines in this section align with the lessons provided in the **Teacher's Edition**, but allow you to take a flexible approach so you can meet the needs of all your students.

Small Group and Guided Reading Routines

- Leveled Reader
- Online Differentiated Genre Passage

Leveled Reader Routine

1. **Preview and Predict.** Encourage and focus discussion by having students read the title and table of contents of the book. Have them predict how the book links to the genre study's Essential Question.

   Read the title and table of contents of the book. With a partner, discuss your predictions about how this book will help you answer the genre study's Essential Question.

2. **Review the Genre.** Review the text features of the Leveled Reader's genre with students.

   This book is a biography. A biography tells the events in a real person's life in order. A biography may include text features such as sidebars, timelines, and photographs.

3. **Have Students Close Read the Leveled Reader for a Purpose.** Each Leveled Reader has a companion graphic organizer that helps to focus students' reading. As you listen in to individual students, choose from the questions provided in the Teacher's Edition as needed to support their understanding.

   As you read, use the copy of the graphic organizer to help you focus your thinking.

4. **Respond to the Reading.** After completing the book, have students complete the Respond to Reading page questions in the Leveled Reader.

   Turn to the Respond to Reading page. Think about the Essential Question and your completed graphic organizer as you answer the questions on this page.

Online Differentiated Genre Passage Routine

1. **Build Background.** Tell students the name of the online Differentiated Genre Passage and explain that it will help them understand more about the Essential Question.

   The title of this passage is "Dreaming of the Stars." As you read it, think about how it connects to the Essential Question.

2. **Review the Genre.** Discuss the features of the genre.

   The genre of this passage is biography. A biography tells the events in a real person's life in order. It also includes text features such as timelines, photographs, and sidebars.

3. **Have Students Read and Annotate the Passage.** Have students do a first read, annotating the text as they read. Use the Read questions to help them focus on text structures, vocabulary, and text features.

   Read the passage, annotating it as you read. Be sure to note the key ideas and details, any unfamiliar words you come across, and any questions you have.

4. **Have Students Reread the Passage.** Have students read the passage again, and then answer the Author's Craft questions provided at the end of the text. The questions will help students dig deeper to figure out why the author did what he or she did and understand how the text works.

   Now reread the passage and answer the Author's Craft questions that follow it.

5. **Help Students Integrate Knowledge and Ideas.** Have students make connections between the genre passage and the other selections they have read. Use the Integrate questions in the **Teacher's Edition** to guide students' conversations.

Additional Strategies for Teaching Small Group and Guided Reading

Managing Small Groups Taking the time to organize and plan will help you manage small group instruction more effectively. You can use the book, *Managing Small Groups*, by Dr. Vicki Gibson and Dr. Douglas Fisher on **my.mheducation.com** to find all the information you need for setting up your classroom, creating rotation charts, and developing procedures that allow you teach a small group while the rest of the class is engaged in productive literacy activities.

Encourage Academic Language Create a chart with academic language related to the strategy you are working on and post it near your small-group area. Encourage students to use this language as they discuss the text and explain how they applied a strategy.

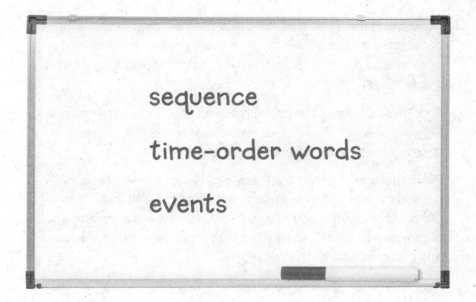

Reinforce With Specific Praise Give students specific, positive feedback when you observe them using strategies and skills well. For example, *I see that you reread that sentence to be sure you understood it. Great work! Rereading is a good strategy to use to comprehend what you read.*

Independent Reading

What You Need to Know About Independent Reading

Independent reading is when students choose what to read. Independent reading time provides your students with the opportunity to apply reading strategies and skills they are taught in class, and helps them make connections with what they are learning. Independent reading can also provide your students with consistent opportunities to build reading stamina and fluency. Independent reading can be part of your center rotation and is an excellent way to engage students productively while you work with small groups.

What students read is based on their personal choice with guidance—as needed—from you. In some cases, especially in upper elementary grades, your students read outside the classroom. However, you may want to provide independent reading as an option during center or independent time. Students can be encouraged to

- read texts on their independent reading level;
- read more complex selections about topics that interest them; or
- reread familiar texts or previously scaffolded texts.

In other words, the books your students choose to read can be easy, at their independent reading level, or challenging but of high interest.

Research

- Research indicates that independent reading increases students' comprehension and builds their vocabulary.
- Studies have found that independent reading of a wide variety of texts also builds students' background knowledge on the topics and concepts which they read about.

> 66 Basically, we should encourage kids to read on their own, they should have a lot of autonomy in choice, and reading level is only one factor in the kinds of books kids should be choosing (and that we should be encouraging). 99
>
> – Dr. Timothy Shanahan

How Does *Wonders* Teach Independent Reading?

In *Wonders*, students read widely across a connected text set, participate in collaborative conversations about their notes and what they've noticed, and write about what they've read. Now they're ready for independent reading. Because reading independently is a big part of helping your students become stronger readers, *Wonders* recommends the following timeframes for daily independent reading:

Grade	Time
Kindergarten	10–15 minutes
First Grade	10–20 minutes
Second Grade	10–20 minutes
Third to Sixth Grade	30–40 minutes

Check This Out!

Independent Reading selections in the Literature Anthology are additional Anchor Texts and Paired Selections not used in the genre studies in Grades 2–6.

There are many opportunities for students to read independently:

- Independent Reading selections in the **Literature Anthology**
- Differentiated Genre Passages
- Classroom Library Trade books with online lessons that include activities for students to complete with a partner or in small groups
- Bonus Leveled Readers
- Online Leveled Reader Library
- Online Unit Bibliography to share with students; they can choose books for daily independent reading and then respond in their writer's notebooks
- Differentiated Workstation Cards
- Time for Kids online digital articles

Teaching Tip

It is important for students to know what to do when they finish reading. Talk with your students about responding to reading in their writer's notebooks or reading log. Make sure there are activities for your students to work on so they don't disturb other readers.

What Does Success Look Like?

During independent reading time, you should see your students previewing books to decide which one to read. They might be reading titles, talking quietly with a partner, or flipping through a book to help them choose. Students should be reading quietly. They might also be participating in collaborative conversations, book talks, or literary circles; responding to what they read; or looking for another book if they are finished with the one they were reading.

Routines

The Independent Reading routines will help assess your students' needs and help them know what to do during reading time.

Independent Reading Routines

- Independent Reading
- Teacher-Student Conference
- Book Talk

Independent Reading Routine

Teach this routine to students so they can choose books and read independently while you work with groups or confer with individuals.

1. Select a book that interests you.

   Check the book to make sure it's the one you want to read.

   See the Five Finger Rule on page 120 as one way to help students check how difficult a book is. See the Additional Strategies on pages 113–119 for more ways to help students choose a book.

2. Read the book each day during Independent Reading time.

   Use the skills and strategies you've been working on.

3. Think about what you're reading.

   You can use Thinking Codes to record your thoughts or write about them in your writer's notebook.

4. Record what you've read at the end of each Independent Reading session.

   Keep track on your Reading Log.

   There are many suggestions for keeping students accountable for their independent reading in the Additional Strategies section. Using a Reading Log is just one way.

5. Share your opinion of the book when you're done.

   Tell a friend, write a review, make a poster, or ask your teacher for ideas.

6. Begin again!

   Time to pick a new book!

Corrective Feedback

Observe students to be sure they are reading quietly. If a student is noisy, check to make sure the book he or she chose is appropriate. Let students know that it's okay to abandon a book that may be more difficult or not as interesting as they thought. Help students choose books that are appropriate.

Teacher-Student Conference Routine

1. Make a positive observation about the student's reading or book choice. Regularly conferring with students about their Independent Reading is a great way to informally assess their progress, model social-emotional learning skills, build your classroom culture, and instill habits of learning.

2. Talk about how the reading is going.

   Why did you choose this particular book or genre? Why did you abandon this book? How is your current book going? Are you using Thinking Codes and are they helping? What strategies are you using and what ones do you need help with? How are you solving problems as you read? Who is your favorite character and why? What is your favorite part so far and why?

3. Ask the student to read aloud for a minute or two. This will help you assess their accuracy, fluency, and comprehension.

4. Highlight a student strength.

   I really like the way you used context clues to figure out what that word means. And adding that word to your writer's notebook is a good idea.

5. Suggest a specific goal the student can work on.

   When you have an opinion, make sure to find text evidence to support it.

6. Record notes from your conference. Use the conference forms on pages 121 and 122.

Book Talk Routine

1. Summarize the story. Talk about the parts you liked best.

2. Talk about interesting words you found.

   As I was reading, I wrote down the word avalanche. *It is an interesting word, and at first I didn't know what it meant. I read on and used context clues to figure it out.*

3. Take turns asking and answering questions.

4. Illustrate your favorite part of the story and tell why it is your favorite part.

   Use the "Steps in a Book Talk" and "Rules for your Book Talk" posters on pages 95 and 96 in the online **Teacher Resource Book.**

Additional Strategies for Independent Reading

Set Up Your Classroom Library You want your students to read independently. Help them to do that by setting up your classroom to include

- areas for students to read, write, engage in word study quietly and independently or to work with a partner or small group;
- access to a rich classroom library, including texts of a wide variety of topics, genres, authors, content areas, and reading levels that are organized for easy identification and selection;
- resources for students to organize their work and writing, including response journals.

Develop a system that works for your classroom space, the age of your students, and your book collection. You might choose to organize books into baskets by author, genre, theme, text type, or topic; display books related to the current genre study theme or topic; or arrange some books by level.

At the beginning of the year, show students how to locate books in your library and demonstrate how to check them out and return them. Make sure students understand when it is appropriate to use the library and discuss how to treat the books with care. Post these guidelines and review as necessary throughout the year. As you acquire new books for your library or borrow new titles from the library, consider doing a book talk to showcase them.

Teacher Book Talks Book talks are a fun way to preview books in whole or small group settings. Hold up the book and give a short, entertaining and persuasive talk about it. Show students where the book will be in the classroom library.

Individual Book Boxes In the lower grades, setting up individual book boxes can help ensure that students are reading each day. You can use a variety of materials: ½ gallon plastic zip-top bags, magazine holders, or cereal boxes cut to size are just a few ideas.

How to Choose a Book Tell students that Independent Reading is a time when they choose what they want to read, and that you can help them make good choices. Share the Five Finger Rule with them and model how to use it as you select a book to read. You can give students the Five Finger Rule handout on page 120 to use as a reference.

Jonathan Kirn/Getty Images

Collaborate With Your School Librarian Librarians are a wealth of information and resources. They can be helpful partners to you and your students as you select books for independent reading and perform research. Here are some ideas for working with your librarian:

- Ask for book recommendations and other resources based on the genre study concepts, Essential Questions, and topics.
- Arrange for a tour of the library and a demonstration of how to find materials and check them out. Ask the librarian to cover expectations for behavior in the library, and review these with your students as necessary.
- Invite the librarian to book-talk new additions to the library to your class.
- Ask the librarian to identify grade-appropriate resources for Research and Inquiry projects and other research tasks.
- Have the librarian demonstrate how to use digital resources available in the library and discuss Internet usage guidelines.
- Schedule regular library visits and help students use their time wisely. Encourage them to ask the library staff for help.

Help Students Respond to What They are Reading

Remind students that readers think critically about what they're reading. They use a variety of strategies, such as asking questions, making predictions, rereading when they're confused, and noting new words. Nurture these habits of learning by encouraging students to keep track of their thinking. Use the Reader Response pages in the online **Teacher's Resource Book**.

Name _____

Reader Response

Title: _____   Author: _____

Rate this book by coloring in the stars.

☆ Awesome ☆ Good ☆ Okay ☆ Disliked ☆ Disliked a lot

Recommendation: To whom would you recommend this book?

_____

Response: Write a new ending to this story. How will it affect the rest of the story?

_____
_____
_____
_____
_____
_____

Reader Response: Fiction   (89)

Journal About Books Students can take notes in their writer's notebooks as they read. Encourage them to record ideas, questions, and interesting or unfamiliar vocabulary words. They can write summaries and personal responses, reflect on their strategy use, and make connections to other texts. Model each type of writing, and periodically ask students to reflect on their journal entries.

Literature Circles Have students reading books about the same genre or topic compare and discuss what they've learned. Keep the groups small and encourage students to think of a question to ask the group.

Thinking Codes To support and scaffold students' journal writing, teach them how to use Thinking Codes to record their thinking in the text using sticky notes. For K–1 students, provide pre-coded notes that can placed in the text. Students in Grades 2–6 can mark their own sticky notes to create a trail of their thinking. Students can then use this record of their thinking as they write journal entries.

Discuss and model how to use each Thinking Code. Use the Thinking Code chart on page 123. Use a Think Aloud to model how you would use the Thinking Codes to show your thinking about a text. On chart paper, write a model entry and talk about what makes it a strong entry. Point out that journal responses should

- show understanding of the text;
- use relevant details and specific, text-based examples and citations;
- cite text evidence that supports the reader's examples and thinking;
- contain key vocabulary and show understanding of the vocabulary;
- contain clear and relevant reasoning;
- demonstrate sequential response.

Share Time A wonderful way to foster a love of reading and build a community of learners is to have your students regularly share the books they are reading. Explain to students that talking about books helps them think critically about their reading and gives them the opportunity to introduce new books and genres to their peers. Bring in book reviews or play clips of online video reviews to demonstrate the authenticity of this activity. Regularly schedule time for students to share books with peers, encouraging students to provide a brief summary (without giving away the ending for fiction), express their opinion, and support their opinion with examples from the book. Here are just a few suggestions to try with your class:

Perfect Pitch Challenge students to present a 1–2 minute "pitch" about their book. The goal of this information presentation is to hook the class and entice other students to want to read the book.

Design a Movie Poster Have students create a poster for their book with the title, author, and a visual that provides a window into the book—characters, conflict, setting, and/or themes. Students can design a poster using pen and paper or they can use an online tool. Have students present the movie posters to the class.

Sketch a Selection Have students stop reading after a few minutes and make a sketch of the most important ideas or details they just read. They can sketch in their writer's notebooks and use them to help summarize the book they are reading.

Get Ready to Talk about Books Have students use the "Book Talks" pages in the online **Teacher's Resource Book** to help them prepare to give a book talk about the book they are reading.

Reading Logs Help students take ownership of their learning by keeping a log their daily reading, noting the date, title, pages and/or time read, and any other information you'd like to capture, such as their opinion or their assessment of the text's difficultly. Use the reading log templates on pages 124 and 125. Model how to fill out the log, and set aside time for students to regularly reflect on their logs and set goals for future reading.

Peer Conferences Provide your students with consistent opportunities to discuss with another student what they are reading. This allows them to exchange ideas about what they are learning and how they are growing as readers. In addition, it offers a valuable chance for you to listen in to students sharing their thinking about their reading with others.

Pair two (or three) students. You might want to group students who are reading the same text or texts on the same topic or theme. Rehearse with students what these collaborative conversations should look like and sound like. By using a gradual release of responsibility, you can ensure that students will be focused when they are meeting with a peer to discuss their reading.

Provide students with specific guidelines to ensure that students will use the time productively. Use the Peer Conferencing handouts on pages 126–128 to model with students.

Highwaystarz-Photography/iStock/Getty Images

Supporting Advanced Learners Through Independent Reading

Independent Reading is a good way to provide opportunities for your advanced learners to develop more complex thinking about the texts they read.

Grades K–2

Author Study or Concept Study Have your advanced learners form an author study group. Have students choose an author. Provide a number of books by the author that you have preselected to show similarities in the author's ideas, writing style, or text structures. Have the group read independently each week and discuss similarities among the books. Provide questions for students to discuss during their collaborative conversations: *How are these books the same? How are they different? What does the author do to help you...?*

Remind students to use evidence from the text and illustrations to support their opinions and ideas. Have students decide on how to present their ideas at the end of the study. If they need support, provide them with the following suggestions:

- Write a response comparing the books.
- Write about a favorite book by the author. Tell why.
- Write an article about the author for a newspaper.
- Write a report about the topic.

Grades 3–6

Author Study Have students form an independent study group and choose an author to study. Have students choose two pieces of work by the author and read the selections independently. Students should have collaborative conversations about their reading each week in which they can

- choose a character and compare their traits;
- compare and contrast themes;
- compare the author's purpose;
- compare text structures;
- compare poetic devices or the use of figurative language and the effect it has on the mood of a text.

Remind students to use text evidence to support their ideas.

Produce and Publish a Movie Trailer Ask students to create a two-to-three minute movie trailer for their books that provides enough plot details to captivate the viewer without spoiling the end. Students can use video editing software applications to create their trailers.

Book Club Chat Have students choose an exciting, interesting, or descriptive passage to read aloud to the group. The passage should reveal something interesting about a situation in the text and/or provide some insight into a main character.

Concept Study Have students do a research report on a topic related to their independent reading. Students may choose to study one of the following topics:

- A specific time-period from a text
- A specific concept or idea from a text
- A specific person in history
- The pros and cons of a controversial subject

Have students decide on how to present their ideas at the end of the study. If they need support, make the following suggestions:

- Write a research report including an organizational structure that supports the research.
- Create a historical timeline of a subject or person.
- Write a biographical sketch of a person.
- Write a persuasive article for a newspaper.
- Create a PowerPoint presentation for any of the above.

Independent Reading Resources

Use the posters, charts, and resources on pages 120 - 128 to help your students become independent readers.

Five Finger Rule

What to do to pick an independent reading book

✓ Choose a book you want to read.

✓ Open the book to any page.

✓ Put one finger up for each word you can't figure out.

0-1 Fingers

This book will be easy for you. Make sure you don't choose too many books that are easy for you.

0-2 Fingers

This is a great choice!

3-4 Fingers

Give this book a try.

5+ Fingers

This is a challenging book. You might want to make another choice.

Independent Reading Conference Form

Student _____ Date _____

Title: _____

Author: _____

Circle One:

Easy   Just Right   Challenging

Conference FOCUS: (Circle One)

Decoding Strategies   Fluency   Retelling

Comprehension   Specific Skill/Strategies

Other: _____

NOTES: _____

_____

_____

_____

_____

Next Steps: _____

_____

_____

Future Teaching Point: _____

_____

_____

Reading Conferencing Class Sheet/Notes

Student Name:

_____

Date:_____

Strengths Noted:

_____
_____
_____
_____

Teaching Point:

_____
_____
_____
_____

Student Name:

_____

Date:_____

Strengths Noted:

_____
_____
_____
_____

Teaching Point:

_____
_____
_____
_____

Student Name:

_____

Date:_____

Strengths Noted:

_____
_____
_____
_____

Teaching Point:

_____
_____
_____
_____

Student Name:

_____

Date:_____

Strengths Noted:

_____
_____
_____
_____

Teaching Point:

_____
_____
_____
_____

Student Name:

_____

Date:_____

Strengths Noted:

_____
_____
_____
_____

Teaching Point:

_____
_____
_____
_____

Student Name:

_____

Date:_____

Strengths Noted:

_____
_____
_____
_____

Teaching Point:

_____
_____
_____
_____

Thinking Codes

 **Favorite Part**
(I love... . Wow!!)

 **Funny Part**
(This is so funny...)

 **Confusing Part**
(I'm confused...)

 **Important Part**
(This is a key detail...)

 **I wonder?**
(Hmmm... I wonder...)

 I concluded...
I figured out...

K-2 Daily Reading Log

Name_____

Date	Title	Genre I or L	My Opinion 😊 😐 ☹️	C Complex E Easy for Me JR Just Right	✔ Still Reading A Abandoned F Finished

Genre Abbreviations
L = Literature, Fiction, Stories, Poetry
I = Informational / Content / Consumer / Nonfiction

3-6 Daily Reading Log

Name_____

Date	Title	Genre Text Type	My Opinion ☺ ☺ ☹	# of pages read	# of minutes read	C Complex E Easy for Me JR Just Right	✔ Still Reading A Abandoned F Finished

Genre Abbreviations

Informational Consumer = **Inf C**	Fantasy Fiction = **F F**	Informational Content= **I**	**Realistic Fiction = RF**
Autobiography = **AB**	Historical Fiction = **H F**	Mystery = **M**	Science Fiction = **SF**
Biography = **B**	Magazine = **MAG**	Poetry = **P- Inf P- Lit**	Traditional Literature = **TL**

Guidelines for Peer Conferences

Peer Discussion

Share your Independent Reading with your partner.
Decide who will share first.

When it is your turn to be the speaker, tell your partner(s) the following:

1. Your book title/ genre	The book I am reading today is _____. It is (genre/text type) _____.
2. Thinking Code you are referring to (or specific strategy/skill focusing on)	The thinking code I left on this page was _____
3. Show page number / text evidence	Here is the page or part I am talking about....
4. Share your thinking as a reader	What I'm thinking is _____ . I was wondering _____ The author here is _____

Guidelines for Peer Conferences

TAG
Writing Conference

T

Tell something you like about the writing.

A

Ask a question about the writing.

G

Give a suggestion of something to add to the writing.

TAG
Writing Conference

T

- I really like how you say…
- My favorite part is…
- What I like about your picture is…

A

- What does that mean?
- What happened next?
- What else…?

G

- Can I suggest you add…?
- I think you need another detail…
- Add to your picture…

Grades 3-6 Peer Conferences Rubric

	Point Value Description	Points Earned / Comments	
		PEER	TEACHER
Date	**1 point** What is today's date?		
Book Title	**1 point** What Text are you responding to?		
State the Thinking Code(s)	**2 points** What are you thinking? What will you write about? What is your focus?		
Page / Paragraph	**1 point** Where is this located in the text? Be specific.		
Reference to and/or Quotation of Specific Text Evidence	**2 points** REFER to KEY DETAILS in the TEXT and/or STATE one or more explicit quotes from the text that best illustrates and supports your thinking code(s) used.		
Your Thinking as a Reader	**3 points** Statements that link back to the thinking code and provide a relevant cohesive conclusion to your response. WHAT ARE YOUR THOUGHTS?		

READING RESPONSE-
*NOTE: All criteria MUST be modeled, discussed, and practiced

Total: _____ 10pts   _____ 10pts

Fluency

What You Need to Know About Fluency

Reading fluency is reasonably accurate reading, at an appropriate rate, with suitable expression, that leads to accurate and deep comprehension and the motivation to read.

- **Reasonable Accuracy:** The student is able to recognize letter names, sounds, and words with automaticity. Students demonstrate fluency when they are successfully able to decode print accurately.

- **Appropriate Rate:** Students can make it sound as if they are talking when they read aloud. Their reading sounds like speech. (See Oral Reading Fluency Norms, Targets, and Assessment on pages 135–136.)

- **Suitable Prosody:** Students can read with expression and phrasing. Prosody develops from acquiring efficient word and text reading skills. Expression is a component of oral reading. It includes pitch, tone, volume, emphasis, and rhythm in speech or oral reading. In some research on fluency, expression is referred to as prosody. Another aspect of expression is a skillful reader's ability to "chunk" words together into appropriate phrases.

Research

- Studies have shown that 75% of students with comprehension difficulties have underlying fluency issues (Duke, 2001).

- Repeated readings should be a part of weekly reading practice. They are essential for all students in Grades K–4, and valuable for students needing support in Grades 5 and beyond as part of a targeted intervention.

- Research shows that comprehension is limited by inaccurate reading (below 95% accuracy.) Comprehension is also limited by slow, laborious reading or by reading too fast. Readers who demonstrate suitable prosody indicate reading fluency by moving beyond mere decoding into expression that likely reflects comprehension. Research states that good reading prosody emerges as children develop efficient word and text oral reading skills. In other words, prosody may be an outcome, rather than a contributor, to comprehension.

> " The hallmark of a fluent reader is one who decodes and comprehends with automaticity. Fluent reading frees up a reader's mental energies from basic decoding and allows a focus on new vocabulary and comprehension. "
>
> – Dr. Jan Hasbrouck

Shutterstock/Africa Studio

How Does *Wonders* Teach Fluency?

Teachers need to model aspects of fluency, including good expression, and then have children apply those skills to connected text. As students encounter more complex text, teachers need to model how to chunk the text into meaningful units for comprehension (e.g., proper phrasing, such as reading a prepositional phrase as a unit or reading the predicate as a unit).

Wonders provides resources for daily fluency practice including Shared Reads in the **Reading/Writing Companion**, Differentiated Genre Passages, Leveled Readers, and Reader's Theatre plays for each unit, available online.

- Fluency lessons have teachers model aspects of fluency, including good expression, and then have children apply those skills to connected text. As students encounter more complex text, teachers model how to chunk the text into meaningful units for comprehension.

- In *Wonders,* echo reading, choral reading, cloze reading, and structured partner reading are effective practice techniques.

  - Echo reading is a reading procedure where the teacher (or student partner) reads the text one sentence or paragraph at a time, then the student (or partner) repeats using the same speed and expression.

  - During choral reading, you and your students read a text aloud together, maintaining the same speed and expression. It can be helpful to use pre-correction prompts, such as "Keep your voice with mine."

  - Cloze reading is when the teacher reads text aloud and the students follow along silently. Every few words the teacher pauses and the students say the next word (a meaningful word) aloud and in unison. This assists students in reading difficult material.

  - During structured partner reading, the teacher assigns students partners. Avoid pairing highest and lowest skilled readers. Consider having the lowest readers work in a small group for practice with the teacher. The teacher designates the amount to read to partner. When an error is heard, teach students to use the "Ask, then Tell" procedure.

    - ASK: *Can you figure out this word?*
    - TELL: *The word is _____. Read the sentence again.*

What Does Success Look Like?

Fluent readers are able to read the text with reasonable accuracy, appropriate rate, and suitable expression. When your students are reading fluently, they are decoding and comprehending simultaneously. This makes oral reading a valuable assessment tool. Fluency should be assessed regularly. A student's oral reading fluency rate (measured in words correct per minute) is a key indicator of reading progress and reading grade-level.

> **Decoding words accurately and ultimately with automaticity is important as students learn to read. Buildling sound/symbol fluency by quick repeated and cumulative review of the previously taught sound-symbol relationships helps students build accuracy and automaticity in decoding words.**
>
> **— Dr. Jan Hasbrouck**

Routine

The Fluency routine aligns with the lessons provided in the **Teacher's Edition** and will help support your students' fluency development.

Fluency Routine

1. **Explain** Briefly explain what reading fluency means.

   Today we are going to work on becoming more fluent readers. Fluent readers read words accurately and make what they read sound like talking. We'll go through examples of fluent reading together.

2. **Model** Model fluency by reading aloud using appropriate accuracy, rate, and expression. First, select a passage from a text. Then select an aspect of fluency to model, such as intonation.

   When we read aloud with natural expression, we show which words go together by pausing, raising and lowering our voices, and emphasizing certain words and sounds. Today, I am going to read a passage from your Student Book. Listen to me read. Notice how fast or slow I am speaking, note any time I stop, make facial expressions, or raise or lower my voice. For example, if I read a question, I will raise my voice at the end.

   Read the passage. Point out the places where you read with expression. Note the phrases or sentences in which you raised or lowered your voice to emphasize or de-emphasize certain words or sounds. Also point out where you paused to show which words go together.

Corrective Feedback

As your students read, offer immediate feedback by pointing out the error, modeling how to correct it, or telling them the word. Ask the reader(s) to start reading from the beginning of the sentence. It is essential for comprehension that students start over at the beginning of a sentence when they make an error and/or stop to figure out a word for a lengthy period of time.

3. **Guided Practice** Echo, cloze, and choral reading are good ways to help students practice correct fluency skills. Select a short passage to read with students. Provide them with a copy of the text.

   a. **Echo Reading** *I am going to read a short passage. I will then go back and read a sentence or two, and you can repeat it after me. Listen to the way I read each sentence. You will use the same speed and expression.*

      (For beginning readers, read one or two sentences at a time and have students repeat. For Grades 2–3, use a passage of approximately 150–200 words.

      As children repeat after you, provide corrective feedback if one or more students reads a word incorrectly.

   b. **Cloze Reading** *Today, we are going to practice cloze reading. Read along silently as I read aloud. If I stop* *reading you all say the next word together.* Pause or "omit" a word randomly, about once every 5–8 words or so. Provide corrective feedback if one or more students reads a word incorrectly or has difficulty with a word.

c. **Choral Reading** *Read along with me as I read aloud. Try to use the proper phrasing, rate, and intonation.*

Use a soft voice so you can hear students, but are also guiding them. Go around the room and notice students who are struggling. Provide corrective feedback if one or more students reads a word incorrectly.

4. **Practice** Structured partner reading is a good way for fluent readers to practice their skills, while at the same time, helping their peers improve their reading skills. After determining the level of fluency among students, pair a slightly more fluent reader with slightly a less fluent one. Make sure that the range in skill levels is not too extreme; otherwise, the more-skilled partner may become frustrated and the less-skilled reader embarrassed. If this happens, partnering will be less productive.

Provide text to your students. *Today, we are going to work in pairs. You will take turns reading the passage aloud to your partner.* The more fluent reader should read first, since they are modeling proper fluency skills. In order not to single out the less fluent readers, assign the more fluent readers a color, such as red. Inform the class that the "red" readers will go first, followed by the "blue" readers.

As children read, observe pairs and provide support by asking:

1) *Were you able to read smoothly?*

2) *Was it easy to follow the punctuation marks?*

3) *Did you know when to begin, slow down, raise your voice, or stop?*

4) *Did you understand what you read?*

5) *Were there any words you did not recognize?*

6) *Did your reader understand what you read?*

It is important that you help each other recognize what you find difficult and what you find easy about reading. Partners should take turns and continue to read for longer times. As an alternative, you can time the readings and have everyone read for one minute.

The online Differentiated Genre Passages contain Partner Fluency Feedback forms for students to complete when partner reading. You may wish to use these as models to make generic forms for partners to use with any book.

Teaching Tips

Provide sentence starters to help students offer appropriate feedback during partner reading.

1) *"That word is _____."*

2) *"Let's say the word together, _____. Now let's go back and return to the beginning of the sentence."*

Additional Strategies for Teaching Fluency

- **Audio recordings** are also useful models for repeated readings and are provided through the ebooks for the Shared Reads, the main and paired selections in the Literature Anthology, and the Leveled Readers.

- **Partner Work** Have students work in pairs to do timed readings of the fluency passages in the **Practice Book**. One student reads aloud while the other student listens and marks miscues. After one minute, the listener stops the reader and marks the last word read. The partners then change roles.

  - Remind student to use context to confirm word recognition or self-correct errors as they read.

  - Help student set up a graph that they can use throughout the year to track the number of words they read correctly per minute.

- **Kindergarten and Early Grade 1:** Early phonics and decoding skills, as well as the ability to recognize words automatically, are the keystones to developing early fluency. At Kindergarten and early Grade 1, offer opportunities for students to practice the following skills with an emphasis on accuracy and building speed. Here are some activities:

  - **Letter Naming** Display letter cards, or use the Sound-Spelling Cards displayed in the classroom. First point to the letters in order, then in random order. As students have more time to practice letter identification, increase the speed with which you point to the letters.

  - **Phoneme Identification** Display upper and lowercase letters. Point to a letter Have children name the letter and the sound it makes. Repeat, pointing to the letters more quickly each time.

  - **Word Automaticity** Have students see how quickly they can identify words. Display a column of 6–8 groups of words. As you point to each word, have students chorally read them aloud as quickly as they are able.

Oral Reading Fluency Norms, Targets, and Assessment

Oral Reading Fluency (ORF) are standardized assessments of reading that have shown to have a moderate-to-strong correlation to reading comprehension and overall reading proficiency. Students read aloud from unpracticed text for one minute. ORF is scored as the number of words read correctly per minute (WCPM).

Research

- ORF norms are the result of thirty years of research by Dr. Jan Hasbrouck and Dr. Gerald Tindal into student ORF achievement. The most recent norms were published in 2017—Hasbrouck, J., Tindal, G. (2017). *An update to compiled ORF norms.* (Technical Report No. 1702). Eugene, OR: Behavioral Research and Teaching, University of Oregon. The ORF norms identify WCPM benchmarks across time and in connection with grade-level percentiles.

Oral Reading Fluency is used for screening and progress monitoring.

- As a **screening** instrument, a student's performance is compared to the ORF norms—WCPM benchmarks at Fall, Winter, and Spring. Student scores in relation to these benchmarks show whether the student is above, at, below, or significantly below results common to their peer group. A student evidencing grade-level fluency should generate a score within a range of ten WCPM above or below the 50th percentile benchmark. Students below or significantly below this benchmark may be at risk. Further diagnostic assessments from Placement and Diagnostic Assessment can be used to identify possible issues in decoding and prosody, leading to decisions regarding leveling, specific reteaching, practice, or intervention moving ahead.

- As a **progress monitoring** instrument, a student's performance is mapped across the assessments (which should be at set intervals) to determine individual improvement or variation in relation to the WCPM time-specific benchmarks. A student's scores will highlight progress, provide data on the effectiveness of any instruction or intervention provided, and offer possible changes to current instruction or intervention options.

The assessments in the **Fluency Assessment** component address both aspects of ORF. They can be administered to screen students at set times to see how they measure up to the benchmarks. They can also be used every unit to monitor progress and determine if students are meeting instructional goals.

- For Grade K and the start of Grade 1, formally assessing oral reading fluency is not recommended. Until children can decode and automatically recognize many words by sight, they cannot be expected to read aloud effortlessly and expressively. However, assessments of letter naming, phoneme segmentation, and sight word fluency are available to assist in determining the types of fluency-building activities and materials to assign.

- Starting with Unit 3, Grade 1 features twenty-four fiction and nonfiction fluency passages that you can use to assess children who can decode phonologically and can automatically recognize many words by sight.

- For Grades 2–6, there are thirty fiction and nonfiction passages per grade to help you assess fluency, using at least two selections every two to three weeks for most students.

Students who are below benchmarks can be assigned lessons from Fluency Intervention PDFs to strengthen weaknesses in rate and prosody.

WRITING
and GRAMMAR

Inspire Confident Writers

Reading and writing are reciprocal processes that enhance and reinforce the skills that students must develop to be college and career ready. *Wonders* emphasizes the importance of reading and writing every day, in every grade, to ensure that even your youngest learners have opportunities to observe mentor writing and take their first strokes as budding writers.

Research also tells us that writing can increase reading strength. There are three writing practices that enhance students' reading (Graham and Hebert, 2010). They are:

- **Writing about the texts they read** — students' comprehension of science, social studies, and language arts texts is improved when they write about what they read

- **Teaching students the writing skills and processes that go into creating text** — students' reading skills and comprehension are improved by learning the skills and processes that go into creating text

- **Increasing how much students write** — students' reading comprehension is directly correlated with how often they produce their own texts

The goal of *Wonders* is to have students become independent writers and thinkers.

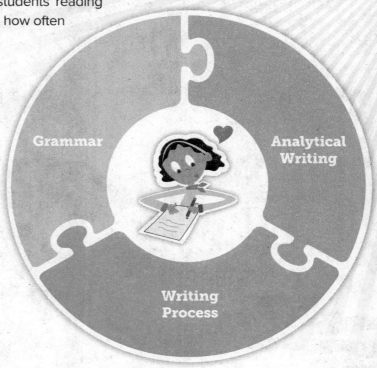

Grammar

Analytical Writing

Writing Process

seamuss/Shutterstock

Wonders provides explicit instruction for each of the following areas:

- In our **Analytical Writing** lessons, students write about what they read. They read texts closely and use text evidence to support their ideas and conclusions about the text. *Wonders* provides scaffolded instruction to help children grow as writers.

- In our **Writing Process** lessons, children learn to write using a 6-step writing process: Expert Model, Plan, Draft, Revise, Edit and Proofread, and Publish. The steps of the writing process can be applied to all types of writing.

- **Grammar** lessons are explicitly and systematically taught each week and are applied to students' writing. Scaffolded instruction allows all students to understand the purpose of using these skills as writers. Students then apply these skills to achieve their own purpose as writers. This allows students to understand the effects of their writing on their readers.

> 66 To be successful in school and beyond, students must learn to write using the information they have gleaned from the text they have read. 99
>
> – Douglas Fisher

Analytical Writing

What You Need to Know About Analytical Writing

Analytical writing is writing about reading. When students write analytically, they summarize, synthesize ideas, and compare and contrast texts. Writing analytically helps students learn to examine and develop a deep comprehension of the texts they are reading.

The purpose of analytical writing is to help your students understand text more deeply. When students write analytically, they take notes as they read. Then they cite text evidence to respond to what they have read. By citing relevant and accurate text evidence, your students learn to draw knowledge from text. And as they begin to write more analytically, they also improve their ability to write their own informational and argumentative texts.

> 66 **Of all the instructional approaches to connecting reading and writing studies so far, writing about text has been the most successful as an avenue to improving reading achievement, and such integrated approaches have been valuable in stimulating higher quality writing outcomes, too.** 99
>
> — Dr. Timothy Shanahan

Research

- Research shows that writing about a text is a powerful way of improving student reading achievement (Graham and Hebert, 2010). Studies also show that writing about a text has a bigger impact on reading comprehension than reading alone, reading and rereading, or reading and discussing the information.

- When students write about texts, their comprehension improves. Responding to reading helps students make connections between what they read, know, understand, and think (Carr, 2002).

How Does *Wonders* Teach Analytical Writing?

In *Wonders*, comprehension and analytical writing are deeply connected. Students write daily following close reading lessons.

When students write analytically, they explore the text more deeply and then use text evidence to write about it. *Wonders* sets the groundwork for analytical writing in Kindergarten, where children share the pen during interactive writing activities. In all grades, students have chances to engage in both group and independent analytical writing opportunities that begin with students using text evidence from their close reading to take notes and respond to text-dependent questions. Students are prompted to write a response or summary or to compare and contrast texts.

We use Respond to Reading writing prompts within the Shared Read and Anchor Text reading lessons. After students read and reread the Shared Read, you model and teach students to analyze the prompt, analyze text evidence, and respond. Students use their **Reading/ Writing Companion** to respond, where they can use sentence starters to support their discussion when they talk about the prompt. Students read and reread the Anchor Text and have an opportunity to use their notes on the graphic organizers and the work they did on the Reading/ Writing Companion pages to write analytically about the text. These Respond to Reading questions require the student to dig deeper into the text, talk about it, cite text evidence, and then write a response.

Analytical writing in *Wonders* requires students to use their annotations and notes. This is important because it teaches students the value of reading with a pencil. Doug Fisher's research has shown that taking notes during reading is useful in analytical writing, as "students consult their annotations to formulate arguments, analyze information, and make connections within and outside the text." But, importantly, he says that students' annotations should have a life beyond their initial construction.

What Does Success Look Like?

As you observe your students writing analytically, you should see and hear students

- circling words and phrases in the text as they read;
- writing down questions and unfamiliar vocabulary words;
- taking notes in their graphic organizer;
- rereading small chunks of text to identify text evidence;
- engaging actively in collaborative conversations about the text.

Routine

This routine aligns with lessons provided in the **Teacher's Edition,** but you can also use it when students respond analytically to any text.

Analytical Writing Routine

1. **Analyze the prompt.** Ask students to work with a partner to read the prompt. Help them identify key language in the prompt and what it is asking them to do. If necessary, define more difficult academic terms in the prompt.

2. **State a clear topic or opinion.** As students talk about the prompt, encourage them to use the sentence starters to help them focus their discussion. Model for students how to use them to figure out the best way to respond to the prompt.

3. **Cite text evidence.** Have students go back into the text to find evidence to support their ideas. Encourage them to:

   a. Evaluate the strength of the evidence as support for the response

   b. Make inferences

   c. Synthesize information

   d. Organize their notes by grouping related ideas or information together

   e. Link reasons for opinions or arguments together

4. **Provide a strong conclusion.** Remind students that well-developed analytical writing ends with a conclusion that restates the topic or opinion. Model for students how to write a strong conclusion.

Teaching Tip

Read the sentence starters and model a response as needed. For Shared Reads, use the Think Aloud provided in the Respond to Reading lesson in the Teacher's Edition.

Corrective Feedback

If students do not cite text evidence in their responses, prompt them to do so. You might ask:

- *What did you read that made you think that? Find the text evidence to support your answer.*

- *Where in the text did the author say that? Show your partner the page.*

- *Which words in the text provide evidence for your conclusion?*

Additional Strategies for Teaching Analytical Writing

Note Taking 101 Use a small group to provide extra support for students on how to take notes. Model using small chunks of the Shared Read.

Think Aloud As I read, I see an unfamiliar word. I will circle the word and write it in my writer's notebook. As I reread, I might find clues to help me figure out what the word means. I will also write down important ideas and details. This will help me summarize the text.

Quote. Paraphrase. Summarize. Model and teach students the difference between quoting, paraphrasing, and summarizing.

- *When you quote, you introduce the quote, include the quote, and then you react to the quote.* Find a quote in the selection. Point it out and ask students to explain what quotation marks are for. Use the online **Grammar Handbook** lessons as needed.

- *When you paraphrase, you have to honor what the author is saying but then put it in your own words.* Read a small chunk of text with students and model how to paraphrase. Have them work with a partner to reread another section of text and paraphrase.

- *When you summarize, you give a more general overview of what is happening in the text.* Explain to students that they can use their notes to summarize text, or tell the key ideas and details.

What's Important? Help students decide which text evidence is important or relevant by modeling and teaching students to gather text evidence in the first few units of instruction. Then gradually release responsibility so that students learn to work independently by the middle or end of the year. Sentence frames are a good way to get students to find text evidence that supports their ideas.

- *I think ____, because on page ____, it says ____.*
- *The text on page ____ proves ____.*

MORE Words Where applicable, remind students to use signal words, time-order words, and descriptive language from the text in their responses. Also, encourage them to use any newly acquired vocabulary while writing analytically in response to reading.

Grammar Connections Encourage students to use the online Grammar Handbook as they write analytically about text. Impress the importance of expressing their ideas in complete sentences, capitalizing the names of people and places, as well as following rules for punctuation.

> ## Quick Tip
>
> For help teaching students to take notes and paraphrase information, see the online videos in Inquiry Space on **my.mheducation.com**.

Writing Process

What You Need to Know About Writing Process

Writing is an activity that overlaps with other processes, such as reading, expressive language, receptive language, vocabulary use, and writing mechanics. The act of writing is rarely linear and requires the iteration of planning, drafting, and revising while simultaneously employing critical thinking skills to analyze, summarize, and evaluate. *Wonders* provides clear guidance for teaching students the steps in this writing process, as well as direct instruction in the skills they need to be successful writers.

Research

- Students benefit from an integrated approach to writing that incorporates elements from direct skill instruction and process-oriented methodology including opportunities for students to engage in writing activities, to apply specific skills in a variety of writing activities, and to participate in peer review and collaboration (Graham & Harris, 1994).

- Teaching students strategies to plan, write and revise is effective for different types of students, including struggling writers (Harris, Graham, & Mason, 2006) and students with learning disabilities (Sexton, Harris, & Graham, 1998).

Shutterstock/wavebreakmedia

How Does *Wonders* Teach Writing Process?

Wonders provides many lessons that follow the steps in the writing process. In Kindergarten and Grade 1, shared writing and interactive writing help teachers model the steps in the writing process and allow students to participate in creating longer writing pieces. Students also write independently.

In Grades 2–6, lessons are provided to support students working through each step of the Writing Process: Expert Model, Plan, Draft, Revise, Edit and Proofread, and Publish. Students learn how to develop real and imagined narratives, opinion/argumentative writing, and informational/explanatory texts. Minilessons provide direct instruction in key writing skills such as organization, adding facts and details, and word choice.

The rubrics in *Wonders* include bullets with specific criteria, and the writing minilessons tightly align to these bullet points. Students are also provided with checklists. The rubrics and checklists allow students to evaluate the quality of their own writing. Anchor papers provide strong models of quality writing, and the student models provide insight into how the writing process works.

COLLABORATE indicates opportunities for collaborative discussions and learning—a cornerstone of *Wonders* instruction. Students work with peers to brainstorm ideas, give feedback on drafts and revising, and help evaluate one another's writing after presentations.

For all grades, the Leveled Workstation Activity cards provide additional writing activities that support each week's instruction. Through these activities, students are spending small group and/or independent time further developing their writing skills.

The Writer's Notebook on **my.mheducation.com** provides a digital pathway that takes students through each step of the writing process. The Digital Tools box also list materials, such as videos and slideshows, that students can use to support their writing.

What Does Success Look Like?

Look for students able to point out the key features of the expert model, follow each step of the writing process, and understand how to use tools such as rubrics, checklists, and student models. Students should understand how to collaborate effectively with peers during each phase of the writing process. Students' writing should reflect their understanding of rubric expectations.

Routines

These routines align with many of the writing lessons in *Wonders*, but you can also use them for other writing that students do.

> ### Writing Routines
>
> - Writing Process
> - Using Rubrics, Student Models, and Anchor Papers

Writing Process Routine

1. **Study the Expert Model.** Analyze and discuss the features of an expert model of the genre students will be writing. These are models that students have already read, discussed, written about, and analyzed during reading lessons.

2. **Plan the Writing.** Brainstorm and choose a topic, discuss purpose and audience, and gather relevant information.

3. **Write a Draft.** Discuss how to develop the topic, organize the writing, and write a draft.

4. **Revise and Peer Conference.** Revise the writing using checklists and partner feedback.

5. **Edit and Proofread.** Edit and proofread revised drafts using editing checklists.

6. **Publish, Present, and Evaluate.** Publish and present the writing. Use a rubric to self-evaluate.

Using Rubrics, Student Models, and Anchor Papers Routine

1. **Review the Rubric, Student Model, or Anchor Paper.** Review the rubric expectations. Examine how the Student Model or Anchor Paper reflects the expectations outlined in the rubric.

2. **Have Students Use the Rubric, Student Models, and Anchor Papers While Writing.** Have students refer to the rubric and models or papers while drafting and editing their pieces. Have students use the rubrics when providing feedback during peer conferences.

3. **Use the Rubric to Evaluate Student Writing.** Evaluate each completed writing piece using the rubric.

Additional Strategies for Teaching Writing Process

Use Writer's Notebooks Tell students they will be writing every day in Writer's Notebooks. They can use the digital notebooks found at **my.mheducation.com** or paper notebooks. The digital Writer's Notebook takes students through each step of the writing process. It also include graphic organizers and links to the **Reading/Writing Companion** pages and other digital tools to help as students write.

A Writer's Notebook can be used for the following activities:

- Writing to prompts every week. Students will check their writing during independent time and make any necessary revisions.
- Completing revision assignments based on writing needs.
- Writing responses to reading to deepen their understanding.

If using paper notebooks, have students write their names on the front of it. Remind them to write the date at the beginning of each new piece.

Then have students turn to the back of their notebooks, and write these headings on separate pages: Synonyms, Antonyms, Idioms, Prefixes, Suffixes, Multiple-Meaning Words, Related Words, Syllable Types. Explain to students that they will use these pages to record words they learn for each heading.

Confer With Students One-on-One Confer with students regularly through each step of the writing process. Use these steps to maximize the potential of each conference.

1. Ask students how their writing is going.
2. Point out something they are doing well.
3. Focus on one teaching point.
4. Connect the teaching point to other writing students might do.
5. Write a summary of your observations and your goals for the student.

Make Additional Mentor Texts Available to Students Remind students of additional mentor texts that are available in your classroom. Encourage them to explore these texts for strong examples of the kind of writing they are doing.

Adjust the Writing Process If Necessary Point out to students that they may sometimes need to return to an earlier step in the writing process. For example, after reviewing a draft with a peer (step 4), they may realize they need to gather more relevant information (step 2) and rewrite sections of their draft (step 3).

Grammar, Usage, and Mechanics Skills

What You Need to Know About Grammar, Usage, and Mechanics Skills

Grammar is the sound, structure, and meaning system of language. The study of grammar includes understanding parts of speech (nouns, verbs, adjectives, adverbs, pronouns, prepositions, and conjunctions) and sentence structure (subjects, predicates, objects, clauses, and phrases). Usage is the way in which we use grammar in speaking and writing. Mechanics involves the conventions of punctuation and capitalization.

Research

- Students benefit from direct, skill-oriented instruction designed to foster text-production skills (Graham and Harris, 1994).
- Teaching skills such as grammar within the context of writing—instead of in isolation—has been shown to enhance writing performance (Fearn & Farnan, 2007).

Shutterstock/wavebreakmedia

How Does *Wonders* Teach Grammar, Usage, and Mechanics Skills?

Daily direct and explicit instruction in standard English grammar, mechanics, and usage is provided in each grade and taught in the context of writing. After instruction and guided practice, students can use the pages provided in the Practice Book for additional independent practice.

After learning a particular skill, students apply that skill in writing activities—for example, as they draft, revise, and edit their work and as they correct their writing in their Writer's Notebook. They can also apply the skill during speaking activities, such as the Talk About It activities at the start of each genre study. Editing and Presenting checklists support students in incorporating the conventions in language as they communicate with an audience, whether through writing or speaking. In Grades 2–6, students can use the **Grammar Handbook** as a resource to develop their own writing.

The Grammar Connections feature in the **Reading/Writing Companion** teaches grammar rules as they apply to student writing.

A variety of interactive grammar games and activities can be found at **my.mheducation.com**.

What Does Success Look Like?

As you observe, look for students who reread their writing and use the Editing Checklist to find and correct errors. Students should be incorporating newly learned skills into their writing and practicing the use of the skill in their Writer's Notebook. Students should also be able to help peers identify issues during peer conferences.

Routine

This routine aligns with the grammar pages included in *Wonders*, but you can also use to teach any grammar skill.

Grammar, Usage, and Mechanics Skills Routine

1. **Define the Skill.** Explain to students what the skill is in a functional and concrete manner.

   In sentences, subjects and verbs must agree. This means that if the subject of a sentence is singular, the verb must also be singular. The bird hops in the grass. *If the subject is plural, the verb must be plural.* The birds hop in the grass.

2. **Explain the Skill's Importance.** Tell students when and where the skill is used and why it is important to use in their writing.

   When you speak and write, it is important to make sure any verbs you use agree with the subject of your sentence. This will make it easier for your listener or reader to understand what you are saying.

3. **Model the Skill.** Write the following sentences on the board. Model correcting them so that the subjects and verbs agree.

   > **Alex eat an apple every day.**

   The subject of this sentence is Alex. Alex *is one person, so the subject is singular. Most singular verbs have an* s *at the end. I need to add an* s *to the verb* eat *to make the subject and verb in this sentence agree.*

   > **The twins swims in the lake.**

   The subject of this sentence is twins. Twins *is plural. To make the verb of this sentence agree with the plural subject, I need to remove the final* s *from* swims.

4. **Guided Practice.** Provide additional practice sentences and model correcting them with students.

   Let's correct the following sentences together.

   > **The bus arrive at noon.**   **The flowers blooms all summer.**
   > **My dog jump when he sees me.**   **Clouds covers the sun.**

5. **Practice.** Use the exercises and activity pages in the Practice Book to provide structured practice opportunities. Prompt students to note their use of the skill when writing in their Writer's Notebooks.

Corrective Feedback

Observe students to be sure they understand how to recognize singular and plural nouns and how to form singular and plural verbs. Refer students to the relevant section in the Grammar Handbook.

Additional Strategies for Teaching Grammar, Usage, and Mechanics Skills

Pumped-up Sentences Write a simple sentence (article, subject, and verb) on the board. Invite students to add to it. They can add adjectives, adverbs, prepositional phrases, and clauses. Have them explain what parts of speech they added to the sentence.

Unscrambling Sentences Take apart a sentence and write the parts on the board. Have students put the sentence back together correctly.

Scrambled Sentence:	likes to chase the dog the red ball
Unscrambled Sentence:	The dog likes to chase the red ball.

Model Sentences Collect exemplars of grammar, mechanics, and usage skills from students' writing. After obtaining their permission, share these authentic examples with the class and discuss why they are effective.

Favorite Sentence Invite students to find a sentence they really like in any text they are reading. Write the sentence on the board, and have them explain what they liked about it. Point out key grammar features about the sentence.

RESEARCH and INQUIRY

What You Need to Know About Research and Inquiry

Research and Inquiry lessons provide students with opportunities to collect, analyze, and evaluate information. They work collaboratively to extend their unit knowledge, practice written and oral presentations, and apply research skills. *Wonders* provides lessons and routines for helping students develop the skills they need to research topics, find and organize information, and present their findings.

Research

- Discussion-based inquiry approaches are significantly related to improved student performance (Applebee, Langer, Nystrand, and Garmoran, 2003).

> " To be successful in school and beyond, students must learn to find information, understand that information, and be able to use that information to support the topic of their writing. "
>
> — Dr. Douglas Fisher

FatCamera/E+/Getty Images

How Does *Wonders* Teach Research and Inquiry?

Each genre study in *Wonders* includes two Research and Inquiry lessons. The first lesson introduces a study skill and a science or social studies research project that students will complete over the course of the genre study. The second lesson provides support for presenting the project. Students can view the online Research Roadmap for guidance on how to apply the five-step Research Process to their work.

In Grades 3–6, Inquiry Space provides the option of having students work on longer projects, following the Online Research Routine made up of six levels that step out the research, writing, and presenting process. These projects give students an opportunity to produce three different forms of writing: informative, opinion, and narrative. Students can work with a partner in or in small groups.

Students also have access to a variety of digital tools in the Resource Toolkit. Tools include animations, videos, and slide presentations to support their research and writing.

What Does Success Look Like?

Students should be able to explain the purpose of each step in the Research Process Routine. They should be able to set goals, find sources, organize their notes, and present their findings clearly and with confidence.

Routines

Use these routines to guide students through collaborative research projects that they share with the class.

Research and Inquiry Routines

- Research Process
- Online Research
- Planning a Presentation
- Listening to a Presentation

Research Process Routine

The Research Process Routine is designed for the Research and Inquiry Projects, but it can be adapted for any research project.

1. **Set Research Goals** Introduce the project and clearly identify the research focus and end product. During this time students may:
   - Generate inquiry questions
   - Create a research plan
   - Assign roles to group members

2. **Identify Sources** Brainstorm and identify reliable sources, such as:
   - Texts read in class
   - Print sources
   - Digital media
   - Interviews with experts

3. **Find and Record Information** Guide students as they search for relevant information from their sources. Ensure they:
   - Take notes from various sources
   - Find answers to their inquiry questions
   - Record information so they can cite their sources

4. **Organize** Help students review and analyze the information they have gathered. They should:
   - Identify the most useful information, by annotating or highlighting their notes
   - Use a graphic organizer to sort and clarify categories of related information
   - Identify any areas where they need further information

5. **Synthesize and Present** Guide students to synthesize their information and create the research product. Then have them plan how to best present their work. Students may:
   - Include audio and/or visual displays to enhance presentations
   - Check that key ideas are included in the presentation
   - Rehearse the presentation

Online Research Routine

Inquiry Space offers students in Grades 3–6 guided instruction on how to complete a formal, research-based writing project by allowing them to independently navigate a safe, game-like digital environment. Guide students through this routine for completing the online research projects.

1. **Analyze the Task**
   - Identify the purpose and audience for the task.
   - Think about the topic and generate key words.
   - Compose a research plan.

2. **Evaluate Sources**
   - Review sources for reliability and relevance.
   - Identify and discard the one questionable or inaccurate source.

3. **Take Notes**
   - Read the remaining three sources for useful information.
   - Take detailed notes while making sure to paraphrase sources.

4. **Write an Outline and Draft**
   - For expository texts, compose a thorough outline that includes a topic sentence, main ideas with supporting details, and a concluding statement.
   - Generate a first draft.

5. **Revise and Edit Draft**
   - Hold a peer conference to receive suggestions for revision.
   - Revise and edit the draft.
   - Cite each source in a works cited page.
   - Proofread the final draft.

6. **Publish and Present**
   - Design an engaging presentation enhanced by visual aids or other forms of multimedia.
   - Deliver a final presentation.

Planning a Presentation

Students have the opportunity to present their research several times throughout a unit. This routine offers a framework for preparing an effective presentation.

1. **Consider audience and purpose.** Have students think about how much their audience knows about the topic, what questions audience members might have, and how researchers can best inform the audience about the topic.

2. **Select audio, visual, or multimedia aids.** Guide students to find or create elements that will help their audience better understand the information being presented. Elements might include visuals such as photographs, illustrations, graphs, charts, or posters; audio such as music, clips of speeches, excerpts from a podcast, or clips from experts; or a video or a slideshow with music.

3. **Plan how to present key information.** Partners and small groups should plan who will present each part of the presentation and who will be responsible for displaying or playing the aids.

4. **Practice the presentation.** Have students use the Presentation Rubric from the Resource Toolkit as they practice their presentation together. You may choose to have groups record a practice session and then evaluate it using the rubric, noting what they need to improve before the final presentation. Alternatively, pairs of groups can practice and provide feedback for each other.

Listening to a Presentation

As students present their writing or research projects to the class, ask the class to take on an active role. Encourage collaborative conversations after each presentation.

1. **Listen actively.** Students should look at the speaker and pay attention. They can take notes about what they're learning.

2. **Think about the presentation.** Students can write down parts of the presentation they especially like. They should write one or two questions about the information that they can ask the presenter.

3. **Share feedback with the presenter.** Students can make comments, ask questions, and listen to the comments of other students.

Additional Strategies to Teach Research and Inquiry

Take a Flexible Approach Be sure students understand that the steps in the Research Process Routine may not be linear. For example, as they find and record information, they may realize they need to re-evaluate a source or perhaps identify a new source. Encourage them to revisit earlier steps in the routines as necessary.

Create a Shared Research Board A Shared Research Board is a bulletin board or wall space in the classroom on which students can place information related to new skills and ideas under study. It is a dynamic space, changing weekly as new information is added. Display the Essential Question in the space, then encourage students to post information about the topic using sticky notes, note cards, sentence strips, newsprint, or other materials. Posts may include

- vocabulary words;
- summaries of or notes about texts read;
- student work samples;
- additional sources of related information.

At the end of each week, briefly review the information on the board. Prompt students to search for an add other information.

Use Rubrics Guide students to use rubrics to plan and evaluate their presentations. See page 159 for a sample rubric.

Presentation Rubric

Rating 4

- Speaks clearly and at an understandable pace.
- Speaks in complete sentences, using conventions of Standard English.
- Uses appropriate facts and many relevant details.
- Presents the information in an organized and logical sequence.
- Uses audio and visual displays to enhance the presentation.

Rating 3

- Speaks clearly for most of the presentation.
- Speaks mostly in complete sentences, using conventions of Standard English throughout most of the presentation.
- Uses facts and descriptive details, many of which are relevant to the main idea or theme.
- Most of the information is presented in an organized manner.
- Uses some visual displays during the presentation.

Rating 2

- At times speaker is unclear.
- Mixes complete and incomplete sentences.
- Uses some facts and details, some of which are not relevant to the main idea or theme.
- Not all the information is presented in an organized manner.
- Lacks clear visual displays.

Rating 1

- Speaks unclearly throughout the presentation.
- Does not use complete sentences.
- Uses few facts or descriptive details.
- The information presented is not organized.
- No visual displays are used.

Ilsegerone/Getty Images

Teaching
EVERY CHILD

Equity in Instruction

In *Building Equity: Policies and Practices to Empower All Learners* (Smith, Frey, Pumpian, & Fisher, 2017), the authors make a distinction between equity and equality, one that is becoming increasingly familiar to educators, district and state leaders, and communities:

> Whereas *equal* means everyone gets the same treatment and services as everyone else, *equitable* means each person gets what he or she needs to succeed... In an equal school situation, we build staircases that learners can ascend to higher levels of achievement; in an equitable one, we make sure to build ramps alongside those staircases (p. 2).

While classroom resources cannot provide equity on their own, they can play an important role in fostering an equitable learning environment, where all students feel supported, encouraged, and empowered. Providing access to high quality instruction and creating the optimal conditions for learning are integral to student success and resolving achievement gaps.

What Does Success Look Like?

Wonders is designed to help support the creation of an equitable and accessible educational environment for every child. All students participate meaningfully in every classroom activity. Our theory of action is grounded in the belief that a high-quality equitable solution provides all students with opportunities to access and fully engage with rigorous, grade-level standards. The resources in *Wonders* allow students to participate meaningfully in every classroom activity by providing teachers with research-based scaffolding strategies that do not compromise rigor or instructional content. Each student receives access in a comprehensible way to both grade-level content and concepts in each unit of instruction.

Universal Design for Learning

Universal Design for Learning (UDL) is a research-based framework for curriculum development that gives individuals with different abilities, backgrounds, and motivations equal opportunities to learn (Rose & Meyer, 2002).

The UDL framework guides the creation of flexible approaches to teaching and learning that can be customized to accommodate individual learning differences. The goal is to customize instruction so that high expectations are maintained for all learners while reducing any cognitive, physical, and intellectual barriers to learning. The three key principles of the UDL framework are as follows:

Representation	**Action and Expression**	**Engagement**
• Perception	• Physical Action	• Recruiting Interest
• Language	• Expression and Communication	• Sustaining Effort
• Comprehension	• Executive Function	• Self-Regulation

Representation

The curriculum must provide many ways to represent content so that different learners are given different ways to learn and integrate the content.

Perception It is important to ensure that key information is equally perceptible to all learners. This is achieved by providing the same information through multiple modalities (e.g., visual, auditory, tactile) and providing information in a format that can be adjusted by the user. The provision of multi-modal learning opportunities and materials has been shown to benefit all learners, including those with sensory and perceptual differences

What does it look like in *Wonders*?

- *Wonders* provides information and content in multiple ways to meet all learners' needs. The curriculum includes a vast array of multi-modal and customizable digital assets to support learners with varying perceptual needs and strengths.
- Digital content for *Wonders* can be visually modified using the controls, allowing the text to be increased or decreased as necessary. Learners can control font size and formatting, as well as background color, when submitting responses.

- Teachers and learners can control all *Wonders* videos by increasing to full screen, pausing and replaying at any time, and turning on Closed Captioning support.

- Text is provided for all audio files, including summaries of the Shared Reads in the **Reading/Writing Companion** and **Literature Anthology** selections. Audio summaries in nine different languages are also included. Files of student materials can be provided to create Braille files and include descriptions of the images found in the student materials.

Language Not only should the alternative representations provide access to content, but they should also clarify key content for all learners as well.

What does it look like in *Wonders*?

- Within the *Wonders* lesson plans, teachers are instructed to model learning strategies and guide students' comprehension of new vocabulary words, noted in bold throughout the text, through pre- and post-reading activities. Daily conversations and writing activities allow students to authentically incorporate the vocabulary, providing opportunities for formative assessment so teachers can ensure students understand the content they are learning.

- The Visual Glossary found in **my.mheducation.com** provides visual aids for all vocabulary words that students are expected to learn. Videos are provided for a subset of the words to ensure that students understand the meaning. **Visual Vocabulary Cards** offer additional visual and tactile support.

Visual Vocabulary Cards

- Digital recordings of all texts, including Shared Reads in the Reading/Writing Companion the anchor texts in the Literature Anthology, Big Books of literature, as well as the Differentiated Genre Passages and Leveled Readers, are available.

- All texts in the core program contain the Audio Text Highlight feature, which highlights grammatical and syntactical chunks of text during the audio reading.

- The Language Transfers Handbook provides cross linguistic transfer analysis to help teachers understand the language of the learners.

- Concept videos and photographs are used to introduce the Essential questions and topics.

Video

- The Inquiry Space toolkit illustrates key concepts through multiple media (e.g., illustrations, simulations, or interactive graphics that make explicit the connections between text and illustrations, diagrams, or other representations of information).

Comprehension All students must learn how to process information that they learn so that they are able to integrate new information with prior knowledge, categorize information strategically, and increase active memorization or recall.

What does it look like in *Wonders*?

As each Essential Question is introduced in *Wonders*, students are supported in activating prior knowledge through

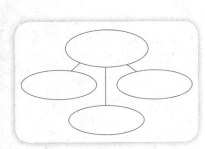

Graphic Organizer

- photographs and videos that help supply or initiate recall of background knowledge.
- collaborative graphic organizers for recording ideas. Organizers allow teachers and students to highlight patterns, critical features, big ideas, and relationships (e.g., use outlines to emphasize important ideas or draw students' attention to critical features).
- materials also guide information processing, visualization, and manipulation (e.g., provide explicit prompts for each step in a sequential process). Instruction is provided for cross-curricular connections students make as they answer the Essential Question through the Connect to Content features.

Action and Expression

Learners differ in the ways that they can navigate a learning environment and express what they know. The curriculum materials allow for multiple ways for students to demonstrate their learning.

Physical Action It is important to provide materials with which all learners can interact. Materials should provide common assistive technologies through which individuals with movement impairments can navigate and express what they know.

What does it look like in *Wonders*?

Lessons are designed to provide students with multiple ways to demonstrate their understanding.

Sound Spelling Song Movement Video

- Students can utilize keyboards and alternate shortcut commands to type and submit responses online.
- Kinesthetic, tactile, and spatial learning activities are incorporated into lesson plans throughout the grades to vary the methods in which students can respond to their learning, such as
  - songs and movement activities
  - phonics activities
  - vocabulary activities
  - Workstation Activity Cards.

Expression and Communication It is important to provide alternative modalities for expression, both to level the playing field among learners and to allow each learner to appropriately (or easily) express knowledge, ideas, and concepts. All learners often need multiple scaffolds to assist them as they practice and develop independence.

What does it look like in *Wonders*?

Students can choose from a variety of ways to respond to *Wonders* assignments, including

- typed responses, completed in one sitting or as saved drafts across multiple periods
- collaborative online work
- oral presentations of content learned

Instruction is presented in multiple media formats to engage all types of learners:

- Inquiry Space projects guide students through a step-by-step process of completing more complex performance tasks. Tasks include an array of multimedia tools to help students evaluate sources, take notes, develop their drafts, and edit their work.
- Research and Inquiry projects offer students options to create projects in multiple media, such as text, speech, drawing, illustration, visual art, and music.
- Graphic organizers are used throughout the close reading of texts for note-taking. They are also used to develop students' own writing in the planning stages.
- Scaffolded support is provided in the differentiated practice for students that need it.
- Independent activities, such as Inquiry Space, Writer's Workspace, and Workstation Activity Cards, are provided for students who are ready for more freedom in their learning.

Executive Function Executive functioning skills are the mental processes that enable us to plan, focus attention, remember instructions, and juggle multiple tasks. The curriculum should focus on efforts to expand executive functioning capacity in students, by scaffolding lower level skills so that they require less executive processing.

What does it look like in *Wonders*?

In addition to researched-based best practices in instruction in reading and writing, speaking and listening, and critical thinking, *Wonders* is designed to build the habits of learning that will help students succeed, such as asking questions, listening to the insights of others, and persisting against difficulties. Teacher resources offer support for building habits of learning in every unit and provide guidance for creating a classroom culture that will further support student success.

In all Grades K–5, *Wonders* integrates key executive functioning processes that will support learning and growth: working memory, focused attention, task persistence, and many more. Instructional routines, which begin in Kindergarten and developmentally progress through the grades, play a key part in expanding students' ability for executive functioning capacity. Routines for applying reading skills and strategies to reading texts, engaging in collaborative conversations, finding and evaluating text evidence, writing about reading, as well as explicit instruction in following processes for Research and Inquiry projects and extended writing, build students' capacity to recall information, plan their work, and complete multistep tasks. The routines and instruction also build students' stamina for completing more complex tasks.

In *Wonders,* students are exposed to each text multiple times before completing extended responses. During the close reading of the text, students' complete annotations based on prompts to guide their thinking.

The Genre Writing projects and Write to Sources assignments walk learners through the writing process and break down the longer writing assignment into smaller chunks. Teachers have the ability to attach specific rubrics to assignments or create customized rubrics based on student needs.

Students can view rubrics and use them as checklists prior to submitting an assignment.

To help students monitor their progress, *Wonders* provides:

- Track Your Progress features in the **Reading Writing/Companion** asks students to evaluate their progress on key skills that they have learned
- Check for Success features in the **Teacher's Edition** that provide timely feedback on the key lessons
- Opportunities to give feedback to students during weekly Teacher and Peer Conferences on their writing
- Writing Rubrics, Student Models, Listening and Speaking checklists to help students reflect on the quality and completeness of their work
- Progress bars on online games help students track their progress.

Engagement

The curriculum allows students to choose from multiple options for learning. Students are engaged or motivated to learn in very different ways. Providing multiple options for engagement is essential.

Recruiting Interest It is important to have alternative ways to recruit learner interest.

What does it look like in *Wonders*?

Teachers have the ability to create and modify assignments based on students' needs and interests. A range of texts might be assigned to a class, giving students the choice of which to complete, or specific texts or writing prompts can be assigned to individuals, in order to meet personal goals.

Inquiry Space

- Research projects allow students individual choice and autonomy in their learning.
- The **Inquiry Space** toolkit gives students discretion and autonomy by allowing them to choose which tools they can benefit from in their research task.
- A variety of tools for information-gathering, such as Writer's Workspace, print and digital Graphic Organizers, Concept Webs, and Writing Rubrics give students discretion over choosing how to gather information.

To increase the value and relevance of their work, *Wonders* provides students with materials that are culturally and socially relevant, personalized to learners' lives and appropriate for different racial, ethnic, and gender groups.

- The **Reading/Writing Companion**, **Literature Anthology**, Leveled Readers, and Classroom Library Trade Books address a broad spectrum of cultural, ethnic, and gender-diverse texts.
- Genre Writing projects have students create personalized, authentic written texts for varied audiences.
- Research and Inquiry projects encourage the use of imagination to answer questions and present complex ideas in creative ways.

Sustaining Effort and Persistence The more that students can regulate their attention, the more they can focus and concentrate on their learning. The ability to regulate attention varies greatly among learners and can change throughout the school day. In addition, students benefit from support in the development of task persistence, especially when tasks are difficult or unfamiliar. Like academic content, sustained persistence is a skill that must be learned and practiced.

What does it look like in *Wonders*?

Wonders provides students with ways to sustain effort and persistence in the following ways:

- With any assignment, teachers can customize the requirements and expectations for the class, custom learning groups, or individual students.

- Modifying prompts, turning on audio readings, and allowing work to be submitted after due dates are ways in which an assignment can be altered to meet learning goals.

- Online To-Do lists help students stay focused with their weekly goals.

- The Inquiry Space provides students with weekly stepped-out goals for each phase of a 6-week research project. To optimize challenges that motivate students, core instruction includes differentiated practice activities to ensure all students are challenged.

- Leveled Readers and Classroom Trade Book libraries provide differentiated resources to motivate and help students meet their goals.

- To foster collaboration and communication, core instruction includes Collaborative Conversations that motivate students.

- Additionally, flexible grouping allows for communication and collaboration to meet weekly goals.

- Speaking and Listening rubrics also help students understand the expectations for group work. To support effort and persistence, students receive mastery-oriented feedback throughout the core instruction with Quick Checks that include supports and strategies for improvement. Weekly teacher and peer conferences in writing provide students with frequent, timely, and specific feedback.

- The online **Data Dashboard** identifies patterns of errors and provides recommendations for acceleration. This allow students to continue to work in a particular area in which they might be struggling.

Data Dashboard

Self Regulation It is important to help students develop their abilities to regulate their own emotions and motivations.

What does it look like in *Wonders*?

McGraw-Hill Education's collaboration with Sesame Workshop focuses on the social emotional skills within the context of literacy instruction. Sesame Workshop, which appears on-page in Grades K–1, has collaborated with the *Wonders* authorship team to develop a comprehensive K–5 scope and sequence for social emotional learning at any age.

- Explicit lessons in Grades K and 1 focus on skills such as self-regulation of feelings, self-awareness, as well as identity and belonging. Development of these skills continue through the grades.

- *Wonders'* focus on developing habits of learning and a supportive classroom culture, with an eye toward strengthening social emotional skills, supports students in developing their ability to regulate their emotions and motivations.

- Student learning objectives are clearly shared at the start of the week and genre study, so that students are aware of what they are going to focus on.

- Integrated instruction, focused on an Essential Question, provides a meaningful context for learning and applying skills and strategies, facilitating student engagement and motivation.

- The Gradual Release of Responsibility model of instruction lets students know that they have the support needed to achieve learning outcomes through teacher modeling, guided practice with peers and teachers, and multiple opportunities with a variety of texts to practice and apply their learning.

- Every assignment submitted is held in a student's binder, along with peer reviews and teacher feedback, allowing the student to reflect on progress and build upon learned concepts. Students can view rubrics and use them as checklists prior to submitting an assignment. In addition, the Track your Progress feature in the **Reading/Writing Companion** asks students to reflect on what they have learned and what may still be a struggle, understanding that they will get the opportunity and support they need to continue working on those areas.

Supporting Students with Dyslexia

What You Need to Know About Dyslexia

Dyslexia is a learning disability that affects approximately 15–20% of students (International Dyslexia Association). Though it is relatively common, dyslexia does not have a singular definition due to the tremendous variance in its presentation. Many academic, educational, and service organizations suggest their own definitions to encapsulate what teachers and parents see so often with young learners: disproportionally poor literacy skills in comparison with the student's overall academic performance level. A student with dyslexia typically struggles with reading and writing but often displays an ability, even a propensity, to learn when there are no print materials involved.

Elementary-aged students with dyslexia often have difficulties in the following areas (Hasbrouck, 2020; Reid, 2009):

- phonological proficiency
- decoding
- reading words in isolation
- spelling
- passage reading fluency
- rapid naming of letters and letter sounds

Students with dyslexia at any age often display frustration with reading, avoidance of reading, and reluctance to go to school, along with social/emotional and behavior difficulties.

Research

- While screening tools for dyslexia exist, the pathway to diagnosis is a process. In classrooms, educators draw from available assessments, progress monitoring, observation, and feedback loops with parents to evaluate students with suspected dyslexia.
- Despite varying definitions, it is agreed that dyslexia is neurological in origin and not "curable"; children with dyslexia grow up to be adults with dyslexia.
- The most effective instruction for students with dyslexia is integrated to include reading (decoding), spelling (encoding), and writing.
- Students reading on grade level can still be dyslexic. Students with dyslexia may use strong coping mechanisms and hard work to disguise their struggles.

- Despite these challenges, most people with dyslexia can learn to read and write when provided with quality instruction and appropriate supports.

How Does *Wonders* Support Teaching Students with Dyslexia?

Students with dyslexia require targeted instruction for their precise needs, and classroom teachers typically find these targeted interventions to be familiar because instruction for students with dyslexia is rooted in evidence-based instructional practices that work for all students. Students with dyslexia do not require fundamentally different instruction; rather, they require more instructional pathways, more explicit instruction (particularly in small groups), increased emphasis on finding meaning in reading, and increased opportunities to experience success to improve educational outcomes.

Wonders is built on instructional best practices to meet the needs of students with dyslexia. These instructional approaches include the following:

Multiple instructional pathways Students with dyslexia typically benefit from teaching, re-teaching, and additional practice to master key components of reading as compared to their peers. A key feature of *Wonders* designed to enable multiple instructional pathways is the movable Teach It Your Way tab. This tab travels through each week and unit with classroom educators, carrying specific notes about minilessons, small groups, independent time, and resources. You are not beholden to one instructional pathway with *Wonders*. Instead, the program recognizes your expertise in determining what students may need and suggests resources to meet those needs.

Explicit instruction in homogenous small groups Small group lessons offer the opportunity to differentiate and focus instruction for students with dyslexia. *Wonders* includes Monitor and Differentiate features that guide identification of students who might be struggling with a skill. Tier 2 level activities are provided in the Approaching small group lessons. Tier 2 instructional lessons and resources for phonemic awareness, phonics, vocabulary, grammar, and comprehension provide more targeted support for students who need reinforcement, re-teaching, or skills practice. The lessons and practice are geared toward the elements of language development that are particularly important for students with dyslexia (foundational skills in particular) and include practice with letter and word fluency, and oral fluency. The alignment of the skills focus between these resources and the core instruction in *Wonders* ensures focused instruction and practice on the prerequisite skills needed for grade level skills.

Comprehensive reading foundational skills taught across grade levels Students with dyslexia benefit from direct, explicit, and comprehensive instruction and practice in foundational reading skills including phonemic awareness, phonics, decoding, encoding, word recognition, fluency, and comprehension. Throughout each week of instruction, *Wonders* emphasizes the structure of language at all levels, from Kindergarten through Grade 5. Weekly lessons teach, reinforce, and review these concepts with students through the year. *Wonders* also includes hundreds of instructional games targeting grammar, phonics, spelling, and syntax, for multimodal practice. Learning objectives are clearly stated each week at Grades K and 1 and for each genre study at Grades 2–5. Explicit lessons that follow a gradual release model include teacher modeling, guided practice, independent practice, and application. Guided and independent practice allow teachers to "Check for Success" and determine where students may need additional focused, explicit small group instruction. Teach In Small Group features identify lessons that teachers may want to teach in small groups to target instruction. Progress monitoring assessments provide data on specific skills and strategies and the Data Dashboard provides remediation suggestions based on students' needs. Refer to the various sections of this **Instructional Routines Handbook** for more detail on the explicit instruction and instructional routines provided in *Wonders*.

> **❝** One thing we know for certain about dyslexia is that it is one small area of difficulty in a sea of strengths. Having trouble with reading does not mean that you'll have trouble with everything. In fact, most children with dyslexia are very good at a lot of other things. **❞**
>
> — Dr. Sally Shaywitz, M.D.

Clear purpose for reading Because reading is a frustration point for students with dyslexia, they need both high-interest texts at their reading level and explicit reasons to read to entice them to work through their frustrations. *Wonders* links Essential Questions to high-quality texts across genres to pique curiosity, cue background knowledge, and present a meaningful reason for students to read and reread.

Increased opportunity to experience success While reading, spelling, and writing can be pain points, students with dyslexia often shine when learning and expression of what has been learned is separated from print. For example, some students with dyslexia exhibit strong speaking skills and excel at drawing connections from the "big picture." *Wonders* includes components that allow students to develop and showcase these skills in tandem with reading and writing.

Strategies for Teaching Students with Diverse Learning Needs

All students come to the classroom with unique learning needs; in some cases, these needs may also include specialized supports due the presence of one or more disabilities. The Individuals with Disabilities Education Act, or IDEA, is a federal law focused on ensuring that students with certain disabilities have the access and supports necessary for academic success. While IDEA covers thirteen specific disabilities, experts often group these and other disabilities across several larger categories:

Developmental/Cognitive

- Examples: Learning disabilities such as dyslexia, Down Syndrome, and autism spectrum disorder, twice-exceptional students

Behavioral/Emotional

- Examples: Anxiety disorder, oppositional defiant disorder

Physical

- Examples: chronic asthma, epilepsy, muscular dystrophy, traumatic brain injury, fine motor difficulties, low tone, seizure disorders, or absence seizures (students "zone out")

Sensory Impairments

- Examples: hearing impairments, visual impairments, light sensitivity, sensory processing difficulties

A number of research-based strategies have been shown to help students with additional learning needs. These strategies may be effective for all students, though some are specifically tailored to certain disabilities. Examples of effective strategies are listed below.

Developmental/Cognitive

For students with memory and cognitive difficulties

- establish and teach rules and routines;
- provide only one instruction at a time;
- have students restate the instruction back in their own words;
- list instructions on the wall or board;
- allow students to review and practice frequently;
- encourage the use of virtual manipulatives;
- allow additional time for students to complete work;
- encourage students to verbalize what they are doing by using words, pictures, manipulatives, and numbers;
- allow students more time to explain and justify their thinking process;
- build in time for repetition and practice;
- provide opportunities for students to explain the concepts to others;
- represent abstract concepts in a variety of ways such as words, symbols, drawings, movement, and acting out;
- create heterogeneous groups so students can learn from and model their peers' behaviors.

ADHD

For students with Attention Deficit Hyperactivity Disorder (ADHD)

- allow students to move around the class. Interactive whiteboard activities or learning stations are excellent opportunities for physical movement while working;
- keep instructions short. Repeat in a different way only if needed;
- give positive feedback often and consistently;
- emphasize time limits for finishing assignments;
- let students know ahead of time when transitions will occur. Help them make the transition when it is in progress;
- maintain classroom routines and schedules;
- allow students to hold a quiet toy while listening and working;
- help students focus on new information by highlighting key points;
- use real-world examples to which students can relate;
- arrange the class to minimize distractions;

- encourage critical thinking by engaging students in active participation through deep questioning.

Visual and Hearing Impairments

For students with hearing and visual difficulties

- move students closer to where the lesson instruction is happening;
- allow students to work in an area of the classroom that is free of distractions;
- include visual clues on the walls;
- use a medium tone of voice when presenting lessons;
- reduce visual complexity by presenting each key part in the lesson presentation separately;
- maintain "one person talking at a time" classroom environment;
- when appropriate, use peers in the classroom that grasp the content to present concepts.

Behavioral/Emotional Disorders

- Keep classroom rules simple and clear.
- Provide clear and simple directions for classroom activities.
- Reward positive behaviors.
- Allow for mini-breaks
- Use motivational strategies such as offering incentives for academic success, celebrate hard work and good efforts
- Emphasize fair treatment for all. Enforce the expected consequences every time, with every student.
- Provide a "safe zone" for students who may need a quiet space to re-center themselves or work without distraction.

Physical Disabilities

- Incorporate Assistive Technologies
- Arrange the room so that everyone can move around easily. Even if a student does not use a wheelchair or other medical equipment, he or she may need extra room to get around in class.
- Set up a buddy system so that another student can take notes for the student with the disability. A paraeducator may be needed to act as a scribe for other in-class requirements.
- Adjust or modify specific assignments. (See information on Universal Design for Learning on page 162.) A student who has difficulty speaking may need an alternative presentation format in place of an oral presentation.
- Identify your student's area of expertise. The student may have become extremely proficient with the computer, for instance, due to the inability to write by hand.

ENGLISH LANGUAGE LEARNERS

Who Are English Language Learners?

The **English language learners** in your classroom have a variety of backgrounds. An increasing proportion of English language learners are born in the United States. Some of these students are just starting school in the primary grades; others are long-term English language learners, with underdeveloped academic skills. Some students come from their native countries with a strong educational foundation. The academic skills of these newly arrived students are well developed and parallel the skills of their native English-speaking peers. Other English language learners immigrate to the United States with little academic experience.

These English language learners are not "blank slates." Their oral language proficiency and literacy in their first languages can be used to facilitate literacy development in English. Systematic, explicit, and appropriately scaffolded instruction and sufficient time help English language learners attain English proficiency and meet high standards in core academic subjects.

> **❝** Effective teachers understand that English learners are studying complex concepts and processing new content in a new language. These students are capable of meeting high academic standards but require adjustments to the way instruction is presented. If their language needs aren't taken into consideration, they risk becoming long-term English learners. **❞**
>
> — Dr. Jana Echevarria

English Language Proficiency Levels

The English language learners in your classroom have different language abilities depending on their proficiency levels. They can be newcomers, beginners, intermediate or advanced/advanced-high, and their abilities may vary in listening, speaking, reading and writing.

The Newcomer Student

Newcomers bring a rich diversity of cultural and linguistic backgrounds to the school setting while facing unique challenges. These students have varying amounts of formal schooling in their own countries, as well as different levels of literacy in their home languages. Newcomers must adapt to a new school system, develop conversational ability in English, learn basic reading skills, while also acquiring academic English and content.

To progress academically, newcomers must have access to high-utility vocabulary from which they can build English language skills. Much of this vocabulary will become a part of their everyday speech when they are given opportunities to converse with their classmates.

Here are some strategies to keep in mind as you build a classroom environment that encourages conversation.

- Provide enough time for students to answer questions.
- Allow responses in the native language.
- Utilize nonverbal cues, such as pointing, acting out, or drawing.
- Use corrective feedback to model correct form for a response.
- Repeat correct answers to validate and motivate students.
- Elaborate on answers to model fluent speaking and grammatical patterns.
- Elicit more detailed responses by asking follow-up questions.
- Remind students that listening is as important as speaking.

The Beginning Student

- recognizes English phonemes that correspond to phonemes produced in primary language;
- is able to apply transferable grammar concepts and skills from the primary language;

- initially demonstrates more receptive than productive English skills;
- produces English vocabulary to communicate basic needs in social and academic settings;
- responds by pointing, nodding, gesturing, acting out, and manipulating objects/pictures;
- speaks in one- or two-word responses as language develops;
- draws pictures and writes letters and sounds being learned.

The Intermediate Student

- pronounces most English phonemes correctly while reading aloud;
- is able to apply transferable grammar concepts and skills from the primary language;
- begins to ask questions, role-play, and retell;
- begins to use routine expressions;
- can identify more details of information that has been presented orally or in writing;
- uses more complex vocabulary and sentences to communicate needs and express ideas;
- uses specific vocabulary learned, including academic language;
- increases correct usage of written and oral language conventions;
- participates more fully in discussions with peers and adults;
- reads and comprehends a wider range of reading materials;
- writes brief narratives and expository texts;
- demonstrates an internalization of English grammar and usage by recognizing and correcting errors when speaking and reading aloud.

Ariel Skelley/Digital Vision/Getty Images

The Advanced/Advanced-High Student

- applies knowledge of common English morphemes in oral and silent reading;
- understands increasingly more nonliteral social and academic language;
- responds using extensive vocabulary;
- participates in and initiates more extended social conversations with peers and adults;
- communicates orally and in writing with fewer grammatical errors;
- reads a wide range of narrative and expository texts with good comprehension;
- writes using more standard forms of English on various content-area topics;
- becomes more creative and analytical when writing;
- communicates orally and in writing with infrequent errors;
- creates more complex narratives.

How Does *Wonders* Support English Language Learners?

Wonders provides whole group, integrated scaffolded instruction at several proficiency levels.

The Spotlight on Language feature helps students while reading texts.

Support for newcomers is at point of use and includes references to Newcomer components.

You'll also find additional support for small group instruction that focuses on helping ELLs understand the meaning of the texts they'll read and apply the skills they've learned.

Teaching Strategies for Language Growth

Teacher Response Techniques

Providing multiple opportunities to speak in the classroom and welcoming all levels of participation will motivate English language learners to participate in class discussions and build oral proficiency. These basic teaching strategies will encourage whole class and small group discussions for all English language learners.

Wait/Different Responses

- Be sure to give students enough time to answer a question. They may need more time to process their ideas.

- Let students know that they can respond in different ways depending on their levels of proficiency. Students can
  - answer in their native language, and then you can rephrase in English;
  - ask a more proficient ELL speaker to repeat the answer in English;
  - answer with nonverbal cues.

Teacher: How would you describe Charlotte?

ELL Response: Very nice. ●

She is nice. ■

She is very nice to Wilbur. ◆

Teacher: Yes. Charlotte is very nice and caring.

KEY

● Beginning
■ Intermediate
◆ Advanced/ Advanced High

Revise for Form

- Repeating an answer allows you to model the proper form for a response. You can model how to answer in full sentences and use academic language.

- When you repeat the answer, correct any grammatical or pronunciation errors.

Teacher: Who are the main characters in the story *Zathura*?

ELL Response: Danny and Walter is. ●
Danny and Walter is the characters. ■
Danny are main characters and Walter. ◆

Teacher: Yes. Danny and Walter are the main characters. Remember to use the verb *are* when you are telling about more than one person. Let's repeat the sentence.

All: Danny and Walter <u>are</u> the main characters.

Repeat

- Give positive confirmation to the answers that each English language learner offers. If the response is correct, repeat what the student has said in a clear voice and at a slower pace. This validation will motivate other English learners to participate.

Teacher: How would you describe the faces of the bobcats?

ELL Response: They look scared. ●
They look scared of the lions. ■
They look scared of the lions waiting behind the bush. ◆

Teacher: That's right, Silvia. They are scared. Everyone show me your scared face.

Revise for Meaning

- Repeating an answer offers an opportunity to clarify the meaning of a response.

Teacher: Where did the golden feather come from?

ELL Response: The bird. ●

It came from the bird. ■

The golden feather came from the bird in the sky. ◆

Teacher: That's right. The golden feather came from the Firebird.

Elaborate

- If students give a one-word answer or a nonverbal cue, elaborate on the answer to model fluent speaking and grammatical patterns.

- Provide more examples or repeat the answer using proper academic language.

Teacher: Why is the girls' mother standing with her hands on her hips?

ELL Response: She is mad. ●

She is mad at the girls. ■

She is mad at her two daughters. ◆

Teacher: Can you tell me more? Why is she mad?

ELL Response: Because the girls are late. ●

She's mad because the girls are late. ■

She's mad because her daughters are late coming home. ◆

Elicit

- Prompt students to give a more comprehensive response by asking additional questions or guiding them to get to an answer.

Teacher: Listen as I read the caption under the photograph. What information does the caption tell us?

ELL Response: Butterfly ●

It tells about the butterfly. ■

It tells about the butterfly in the meadow. ◆

Teacher: What did you find out about the butterfly?

ELL Response: It has nectar. ●

It drinks a lot of nectar. ■

It drinks nectar from every flower. ◆

Teacher: Yes. The butterfly drinks nectar from the flower.

Educating English Language Learners

Seven Principles to Help Your Students

Wonders also reflects seven principles outlined in the latest research from a concensus report released by the National Academies of Sciences, Engineering, and Medicine.

Here is *Wonders* author Dr. Diane August's explanation of the principles.

1. **Provide Access to Grade-Level Content.** Exposure to the grade-level content provides crucial access to the language required for academic achievement and for becoming fully proficient in English.

2. **Build on Effective Practices Used with English Proficient Students.** Instruction of phonemic awareness, phonics, and read alouds doesn't need to be different. However, ELLs benefit from scaffolded instruction from the teacher when discussing complex texts.

3. **Provide Supports to Help ELLs Master Core Content and Skills.** Visual supports include pictures, short videos, and graphic organizers to represent complex vocabulary and concepts. Verbal supports include student glossaries, words glossed in context, and partner discussions that focus in part on clarifying key ideas.

   For newcomers, core content provided in their home language will support them in developing and acquiring proficiency in English.

4. **Develop ELLs' Academic Language.** Academic language is defined as language used in school, in written communications, in public presentations, and in formal settings. However, academic language differs across content areas.

5. **Encourage Peer-to-Peer Learning Opportunities.** One of the key principles of instruction in a second language is enabling students to interact via speaking, listening, reading, and writing with peers in their second language. Speaking is important to generate feedback and encourage syntactic process.

6. **Capitalize on Student's Home Language, Knowledge, and Cultural Assets.** Ways to do this include providing opportunities for students to engage in conversational exchanges that permit some interpretation to take place in their first language, giving first-language definitions for the targeted vocabulary, teaching word-learning strategies that help ELLs uncover the meanings of cognates, and connecting key concepts to students' prior knowledge or experiences at home and in their community.

7. **Screen for Language and Literacy Challenges, Monitor Progress, and Support ELLs Who are Struggling.** ELLs have been both overidentified and underidentified as having a disability, which is problematic. Measures used to assess ELLs for reading and language challenges must distinguish language development from disability.

Language and Content Objectives

What Are Language and Content Objectives?

A language objective is a learning goal related to language. Language objectives are the *what*—What students need to learn about English in order to

- learn, share, or apply new information;
- demonstrate knowledge;
- perform academic tasks.

Content objectives are the *what*, too—what students need to learn about the content topic.

Teachers should copy the language objective and display it for students for each lesson. Language objectives need to be worded in a way that students will understand.

How to Create Them

Because the language of the standards is very broad, there is some flexibility in writing the objectives. However, it is important to follow the criteria below.

- ALWAYS begin with "Students will."
- Choose language and content-specific vocabulary that expresses ideas precisely and concisely.

Here are some verbs to use to write language objectives:

discuss	write	evaluate
define	cite	analyze
listen to/for	explain	generate
compare	identify	
persuade	determine	

> 66 Language objectives provide focused practice with the vocabulary, language structures, and language skills necessary for developing English proficiency. 99
>
> — Dr. Jana Echevarria

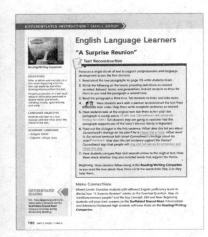

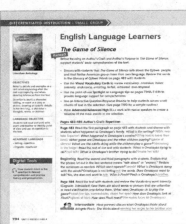

The objectives should work in tandem with English Language Arts content objectives. Here's an example.

ELA Standard: Writing

Write informative compositions in a variety of forms. Choose language and content-specific vocabulary that express ideas precisely and concisely, recognizing and eliminating wordiness and redundancy.

Content Objective: Students will edit a peer's rough draft to identify overused or vague words.

Language Objective: Partners (writer and editor) will discuss the selected words to generate and evaluate alternatives with more precision, description, or sensory detail.

In *Wonders*, objectives appear at point of use in all whole group lessons. In addition, language objectives are included on every small group ELL lesson.

Differentiated Texts

Research shows that for English language learners, exposure to grade-level content provides crucial access to the language required for academic achievement and for becoming fully proficient in English. Because grade-level materials are challenging for ELLs, instruction must be coupled with methods that support ELLs.

Wonders provides scaffolded texts to support ELLs at various levels of proficiency, as well as opportunities for students to Level Up. **Teacher's Edition** lessons provide opportunities for oral language development. In this collaborative environment, students can connect what they already know to grade-level content in order to acquire new knowledge and build literacy. The Scaffolded Shared Reads, Leveled Readers, and Differentiated Genre Passages allow you to

- ensure equity of access to core content;
- prepare English language learners for success through language development.

Scaffolded Shared Read, Grades 2–5: These texts are designed to help Beginning and Early Intermediate ELL students build their listening, speaking, reading, and writing skills in English. Students at the Beginning and Early Intermediate level read a scaffolded version of the core Shared Read and collaborate with partners to answer questions. This interactive set-up provides opportunities for oral language development.

Complete the Shared Read in chunks, instead of truncated text, so students read the same content as core text.

Each Scaffolded Share Read includes these features:

- **Glossary** with definitions in context for challenging words and phrases and translations for each entry
- **Main/Guiding Question** provides purpose for reading each text chunk
- **Additional Questions** prompt students to identify details and specific information to help them answer the Main Question
- **Main Question Revisited** provides students to answer the Main Question in their own words
- **Word Banks** for students to use to help them answer Additional and Main Questions

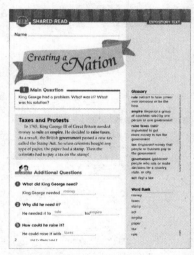

Scaffolded Shared Read

- **Sentence Frames** provide gradual support to help students apply key concepts and language structure to use vocabulary in context
- **Apply Comprehension Skill** by rereading and taking notes on a graphic organizer
- **Summarize** the text collaboratively with peers
- Variety of text features, such as maps, diagrams, charts, and sidebars, to familiarize students on how to use them
- Students create their own Glossary of words and phrases they encounter in each selection

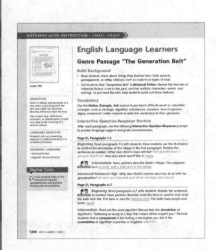

Differentiated Genre Passages Leveled texts targeting Intermediate language proficiency level that helps students read the same core content and apply reading skills: vocabulary strategy, comprehension skill, text features. The **Teacher's Edition** includes Small Group instruction to support these texts at three levels of language proficiency.

Each Differentiated Genre Passage lesson includes these features

- Build Background;
- Vocabulary;
- Interactive Question-Response Routine;
- Respond to Read;
- Make Connections;
- Level Up feature.

ELL Leveled Reader These readers are sheltered versions of On Level texts, targeting Intermediate language proficiency level.

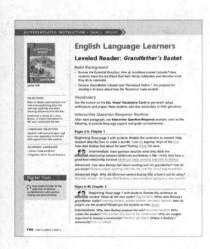

The ELL Leveled Readers include differentiated supports such as

- Labels;
- Stop and Check;
- In Other Words provides definitions and translations in Spanish to aid in comprehension;
- Language Detective to practice applying a grammar skill;
- Level Up feature.

Collaborative
Conversations COLLABORATE

Student Prompts and Response Frames

The chart below provides prompt and response frames that will help students at different language proficiency levels interact with each other in meaningful ways in partner, small group and class discussions. You may want to post these frames in the classroom for student reference. Also remind students to follow turn-taking rules during all discussions.

CORE SKILLS	PROMPT FRAMES	RESPONSE FRAMES
Elaborate and Ask Questions to Request Clarification	Can you tell me more about it? Can you give some details on...? Can you be more specific? What do you mean by...? How/Why is that important?	I think it means that... In other words... It's important because... It means that... In other words... It's important because... It's similar to when...
Support Ideas with Text Evidence	Can you give any examples from the text? What are some examples from other texts? What evidence do you see for that? How can you justify that idea? Can you show me where the text says that?	The text says that... An example from another text is... According to... Some evidence that supports that is...

Build On and/ or Challenge Partner's Idea	What do you think of the idea that...? Can we add to this idea? Do you agree? What are other ideas/ points of view? What else do we need to think about? How does that connect to the idea...?	I would add that... I want to follow up on your idea... Another way to look at it is... What you said made me think of...
Paraphrase	What do we know so far? To recap, I think that... I'm not sure that was clear. How can we relate what I said to the topic/ question?	So, you are saying that... Let me see if I understand you... Do you mean that...? In other words... It sounds like you are saying that...
Determine the Main Idea and Supporting Details	What have we discussed so far? How can we summarize what we talked about? What can we agree upon? What are the main points or ideas we can share? What relevant details support the main points or ideas? What key ideas can we take away?	We can say that... The main idea seems to be... As a result of this conversation, we think that we should... The evidence suggests that...

Cognates and Language Transfers

What You Need to Know About Cognates

Cognates are words that have similar spellings, meanings, and sometimes similar pronunciations across two languages. They make up one-third to one-half of the words in languages that share cognates with English, such as Spanish, French, and Portuguese. Some of the cognates may be technical terms and therefore unknown to students in both languages (hypothesis/hipótesis) Cognates are often useful in promoting comprehension for students whose native language has a Latin base.

For example, using "calculate the mass/volume ratio" may be easier for some students to understand than "figure out the mass/volume ratio" as "calcular" is a Spanish cognate.

Research studies indicate that—under some circumstances—English learners whose first language shares cognates with English are able to draw on first language knowledge to figure out the meanings of cognates in their second language.

Although in most cases cognate knowledge is helpful, in some cases it may result in English learners inferring the wrong meaning of unknown words. Some words are false cognates: they look and sound alike in both languages but do not have any of the same meanings. For example: pie/*pie* (*foot* in Spanish). Or they may share some meanings but not the meaning required in a particular context.

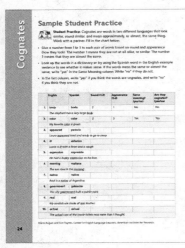

How to Teach Students to Use Cognates

1. Show cognate word pairs and images on a an interactive whiteboard or screen (liberty/*libertad*).

2. Explain that these words are cognates. They are in two different languages, but they look similar, sound similar, and mean approximately the same thing.

3. Model differences and similarities for liberty and *libertad*. (They have many of the same letters, but some letters are different.)

4. Ask a native Spanish speaker to say liberty and compare the sounds in *libertad*. (The consonants are similar, but some of the vowels and the ending sound different.)

5. Have students engage in partner talk. Have them look at the words liberty/*libertad* and disagreeable/*desagradable*. *Which letters are the same? Do the words sound similar enough that you would recognize they may be related?*

6. Explain to students that when they encounter a word they don't know, but it has lots of the same letters and sounds the same as a word in their language, it may be a cognate. However, they should check to see if the meaning of the word in their native language makes sense in the English sentence that includes the cognate. It is always important to then check a dictionary.

7. Explain to students that words can have multiple meanings. Not all meanings of a cognate will be the same in both languages. Remind them that they also need to watch out for false cognates, which are words that sound the same and/or are spelled the same, but have different meanings, such as (pie/*pie*).

8. Give students an opportunity to practice. Have them use the table in the student chart to practice checking words for cognate status on page 24.

What You Need to Know About Language Transfers and Nontransferable Skills

It is important to keep in mind that many skills and concepts transfer from students' first language to their second, and that ELLs may have already acquired core content in their first language. If students have learned math concepts in their first language, they do not need to relearn the concepts, but they do need to learn the English academic language associated with them.

To read and speak fluently in English, English language learners need to master a wide range of phonemic awareness, phonics, and word study skills.

English language grammar differs widely from that of many other languages. For example, a student's primary language may use a different word order than English does, may not use parts of speech in the same way, or may use different verb tenses.

The Sounds and Phonics and the Grammar Transfers Charts in the Language Transfer Handbook, are designed to help you anticipate possible transfer errors in pronouncing or perceiving English sounds, and in speaking and writing in standard English. With all grammar exercises, the emphasis is on oral communication, both as a speaker and listener. The reference to the Language Transfer Handbook appears at point of use in the **Teacher's Edition**. See Phonics and Grammar routines on page x.

How to Use the Grammar Transfer Charts

1. **Highlight Transferable Skills** If the grammar skill transfers from the student's native language to English and that language group is the only one being taught, state that it transfers during the first few sessions. In many grammar lessons, an English learner feature will indicate which skills do and do not transfer.

2. **Preteach Non-Transferrable Skills** Prior to teaching a grammar lesson, check the chart to determine if the skill transfers from the student's native language into English. If it does not, preteach the skill during Small Group time. Provide sentence frames and ample structured and unstructured opportunities to use the skill in spoken English. Students need to talk, talk, and talk some more to master these skills. Use songs, games, rhymes, short skits, and poems to supplement the frames.

3. **Provide Additional Practice and Time** If the skill does NOT transfer from the student's native language into English, the student will require more time and practice mastering it. Continue to review the skill during Small Group time. Use the additional resources, such as the grammar lessons in the Language Development Kits, in upcoming weeks. Include the skill in the reviewing that you do for the class as a whole so English learners do not feel singled out when you do class work.

4. **Use Contrastive Analysis** When you are teaching a single language group, tell students when a skill does not transfer and include contrastive analysis work to make the students aware of how to correct their speaking and writing for standard English. For example, when a student uses an incorrect grammatical form, write the student's sentence on a WorkBoard. Then write the

correct English form underneath. Explain the difference between the student's native language and English. Have the student correct several other sentences using this skill.

5. **Increase Writing and Speaking Opportunities** Increase the amount of structured writing and speaking opportunities for students needing work on specific grammatical forms. Sentence starters and paragraph frames such as those found in the lessons, are ideal for both written and oral exercises. Plays, memorizing short poems, focused conversations, and song lyrics are other ways of doing this.

6. **Focus on Meaning** Always focus on the meaning of sentences in all exercises.

As students improve and fine-tune their English speaking and writing skills, work with students on basic comprehension of spoken and written English.

How to Use the Phonics Transfer Charts

1. **Highlight Transferrable Skills** If the phonics skill transfers from the student's primary language to English, state that during the lesson. In most lessons an English language learner feature will indicate which sounds do and do not transfer in specific languages.

2. **Preteach Non-Transferrabale Skills** Prior to teaching a phonics lesson, check the chart to determine if the sound and/or spelling transfers from the student's primary language into English. If it does not, preteach the sound and spelling during Small Group time. Focus on articulation, using the backs of the small **Sound-Spelling Cards** and the minimal contrast activities provided.

3. **Provide Additional Practice and Time** If the skill does NOT transfer from the student's primary language into English, the student will require more time and practice mastering the sound and spellings. Continue to review the phonics skill during Small Group time in upcoming weeks until the student has mastered it. Use the additional resources, such as the extra decodable stories in the **Teacher's Resource Book**, to provide oral and silent reading practice.

Language Transfers Handbook

Routines

The consistency and predictability of instructional routines can help students feel competent and autonomous. They also allow students to focus their attention on learning and save you instructional time.

Instructional Routines

- Interactive Question-Response
- Define/Example/Ask
- Text Reconstruction
- Scaffolded Shared Read

Interactive Question-Response Routine

This conversational, interactive instruction creates context and provides opportunities for English language learners to learn how information builds and connects. It focuses on key skills, strategies, concepts, and vocabulary. The interactive scripts help students use what they know as they add new knowledge and provide ample opportunities for ELLs to speak and use new language learned. You can use this routine with the Shared Reads, the Anchor Texts, the **Leveled Readers**, the **Genre Passages**, the **Literature Big Books**, and the **Interactive Read Alouds**.

1. After each paragraph, ask questions that help students understand the meaning of the text.

2. Have students discuss the text after each paragraph.

3. Explain difficult or unfamiliar concepts and words.

4. Provide sentence starters/frames for Beginning and Intermediate students.

5. Have Advanced and Advanced-High students retell the information.

6. Reinforce the meaning of new vocabulary.

7. Ask questions that require students to use the newly acquired vocabulary.

8. Use the images and other text features to aid students' comprehension.

9. Reinforce weekly strategies and skills through modeling and questions.

10. Use the subheads and bold print to help students predict what the sections will be about.

Define/Example/Ask Vocabulary Routine

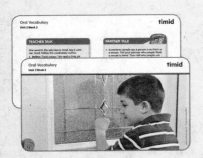

Visual Vocabulary Cards

Use the **Visual Vocabulary Cards** to preteach ELL vocabulary words. Follow the vocabulary routine on the back of the card. Here is an example of using the routine to teach the word *recent*.

1. **Define:** *Recent* means something happened a short time ago. En espanol, recent quiere decir "reciente, ocurrido hace poco." *Recent* in English and *reciente* in Spanish are **cognates.** They sound and mean the same thing in both languages.

2. **Example:** Mary learns about recent events from the newspaper. En espanol: Mary se enteró de los recientes eventos por el periódico.

3. **Ask:** What word is the opposite of *recent*?

4. Now let's look at a picture that shows the word *recent*. Point to the girl. This girl likes to read the newspaper. It tells her about recent events, or events that happened a short time ago.

Partner Talk activities provide strategies to get students talking and using the new language.

Text Reconstruction Routine

You can use the Text Reconstruction Routine to support students' language development and comprehension in listening, speaking, reading, and writing. Focus on a single chunk of text.

1. Read aloud paragraph 2 on page 134 in "Mysterious Oceans" while students just listen.

2. Write the following words and phrases on the board, providing definitions as needed: *creatures, survive, food sources, as a result, adapt.* Instruct students to listen for the words while you read the page a second time.

3. **COLLABORATE** Read the page a third time while students listen and take notes.

4. Have partners work together to reconstruct the text from their notes. Help them write complete sentences as needed.

5. Have students look at the original text and tell what the paragraph is about. (why animals have to adapt to an environment with little food) Tell them that they are going to analyze the author's use of cause and effect to tell about creatures in the deep ocean.

6. Have students scan the paragraph and tell what phrase signals a cause and effect relationship. (as a result) *Is* as a result *a cause or an effect?* (effect) *Which sentence tells the cause?* (third sentence) Discuss the causes. *Which sentence tells the events?* (fourth/last sentence) Discuss the effect.

7. Have students compare their text reconstructions to the original text. Have them check if they included words that signal a cause and effect relationship.

Scaffolded Shared Read Routine

You can use the ELL Scaffolded Shared Read Routine to support students who are at the Beginning and Early Intermediate levels. However, it can be used with all students. This routine aligns with the lessons provided in the online Teacher's Guide and will help support your students' language development.

1. Review the language objectives to make students aware of what they need to learn.

2. Build background by telling students information they need to understand the text.

3. Read the Main or Guiding Question with students to ensure comprehension.

4. Have students read one chunk of text.

5. Use the Interactive Question-Response Routine for each chunk of the text.

6. Have students listen and follow along as you read the text

7. Use the friendly definitions from the Glossary to restate sentences with words students may not know. For example, for the word *existed,* say: *We knew giant squids existed from discovering their corpses. Existed means were present.*

8. Point out the cognates. Write the pairs on the board: existed/ *excistió.*

9. You may wish to review irregular verbs in the text such as *found.*

10. Have partners work together to answer the Main Question.

Additional Activities for Oral Language Development

You can use the following pages for practice.

Conversation Starters

Hello, I'm
_____.

What's your name?

What country are you from?

I'm from
_____.

How old are you?

I'm _____ years old.

I like _____ because _____.

I don't like _____ because _____.

Copyright © McGraw-Hill Education

Conversation Starters

What are you doing?	I'm _____ and _____.
How do you feel?	I'm _____.
Where do you live?	I live in _____.
What's your phone number?	My number is _____.

Oral Language Sentence Frames

Adapting Language Choices

Use the examples and the sentence frames for oral language practice.

Talking to an Adult	Talking to a Peer
Would you please repeat that, Ms. Sanchez? Thank you for the book, Grandma. Mr. Wong, may I please get a drink of water?	What did you say, Annie? Loved the book, Henry. Thanks. Hey, Luis, can I have some juice?
● Would you please _____, Mr./Ms. _____?	● What did you _____, _____?
■ Thank you for _____, _____.	■ Loved the _____, _____. Thanks.
◆ Mr./Ms. _____, may I please _____?	◆ Hey, _____ can I _____?

Oral Language Sentence Frames

Asking Relevant Questions

Use these sentence frames for oral language practice.

What does _____ mean?

Why does _____?

Why does the character _____?

Why does the author _____?

Where does the author say _____?

What does the author mean by _____?

Affirming Others

Use these sentence frames for oral language practice.

I like _____.

Your idea about _____ is good.

I like _____'s idea about _____.

I agree with _____ about _____.

_____ is a good idea.

I agree that _____.

References

American College Testing (ACT). (2006). *Reading: Between the lines*. Iowa City, IO: American College Testing. **https:///www.act.org/research/policymakers/reports/reading.html**

Applebee, A. (1996). *Curriculum as conversation: Transforming traditions of teaching and learning.* Chicago: University of Chicago Press.

Applebee, A., Langer, J., Nystrand, M., Gamoran, A. (2003). Discussion-based approaches to developing understanding: Classroom instruction and student performance in middle and high school English. *American Educational Research Journal, 40*(3) 685–730.

August, D., Branum-Martin, L., Cardenas-Hagan, E. & Francis, D. (2009). The Impact of an instructional intervention on the science and language Learning of middle grade English language learners. *Journal of Research on Educational Effectiveness. 2.* 345–376.

August, D., & Shanahan, T. (2006). *Developing literacy in second-language learners: Report of the National Literacy Panel on language-minority children and youth.* Mahwah, NJ: Lawrence Erlbaum Associates.

August, D., Shanahan, T., & Escamilla, K. (2009). English language learners: Developing literacy in second-language learners—Report of the National Literacy Panel on language-minority children and youth. *Journal of Literacy Research, 41*(4), 432–452. https://doi.org/10.1080/10862960903340165

Bear, D., Academic Vocabulary Study: Embedded, Deep, and Generative Practices. McGraw Hill Education, **mhereadingwonders.com**

Bear, D., Invernizzi, M., Templeton, S., & Johnston, F. (2008). *Words their way: Word study for phonics, vocabulary, and spelling instruction.* Upper Saddle River, NJ: Pearson.

Beck, I., & McKeown, M. (2001). Text talk: Capturing the benefits of read-aloud experiences for young children. *Reading Teacher, 55* (1), 10–20.

Blevins, W. (2000). *Phonics A-Z.* New York: Scholastic.

Carlo, M., August, D., McLaughlin, B., Snow, C., Dressler, C., Lippman, D., Lively, T., & White, C. (2004). Closing the gap: Addressing the vocabulary needs of English language learners in bilingual and mainstream classrooms. *Reading Research Quarterly, 39*(2), 188–206.

Corson, D. (1997). The learning and use of academic English words. *Language Learning, 47*(4), 671–718.

Coxhead, A. (2000). A new academic word list. *TESOL Quarterly, 34*(2), 213–238.

Cunningham, P. (2005). If they don't read much, how they ever gonna get good? *The Reading Teacher, 59*(1), 88–90.

Fry, Fountoukidis, & Polk. (1985). *The new reading teacher's book of lists.* Upper Saddle River, NJ: Prentice-Hall.

Graham, S., & Harris, K. (1994). The effects of whole language on children's writing: A review of literature. *Educational Psychologist, 29*(4), 187–192.

Graham, S., & Hebert, M. (2010). *Writing to read: Evidence for how writing can improve reading.* New York: Carnegie Corporation. **http://www.all4ed.org/files/WritingToRead.pdf**

Hasbrouck, J., & Tindal, G. (2017). *An update to compiled ORF norms. (Technical Report No. 1702).* Eugene, OR: Behavioral Research and Teaching, University of Oregon.

Kamil, M., & Hiebert, E. (2005). Teaching and learning vocabulary: Perspectives and persistent issues. In E. H. Hiebert and M. L. Kamil (Eds.), *Teaching and learning vocabulary: Bringing research to practice* (pp. 1–23). Mahwah, NJ: Lawrence Erlbaum.

Lubliner, S. & Grisham, D. L. (2012). Cognate strategy instruction: Providing powerful literacy tools to Spanish-speaking students. In J. Fingon & S. Ulanov (Eds.), *Learning from culturally and linguistically diverse classrooms: Promoting success for all students* (pp. 105–123). New York: Teachers College Press.

Lubliner, S. & Hiebert, E. (2011). An analysis of English-Spanish cognates as a source of general academic language. *Bilingual Research Journal, 34*(1), 76–93.

International Dyslexia Association. (2018). Dyslexia basics. Retrieved December 7, 2018 from **https://dyslexiaida.org/fact-sheet-5/.**

Murphy, Wilkinson, Soter, Hennessey, & Alexander. (2009). Examining the effects of classroom discussion on students' comprehension of text: A meta-analysis. *Journal of Educational Psychology, 101,* 740–764.

Nagy, W., Berninger, V. and Abbott, R. (2006). Contributions of morphology beyond phonology to literacy outcomes of upper elementary and middle school students. *Journal of Educational Psychology, 98,* 134–147.

Nagy, W. (2007). Metalinguistic awareness and the vocabulary-comprehension connection. In: Wagner, R, Muse, A, Tannenbaum, K. (Eds.). *Vocabulary acquisition: Implications for reading comprehension.* New York: Guilford Press.

National Institute of Child Health and Human Development (NICHHD). (2000). *National Reading Panel—Teaching children to read: Reports of the subgroups* (NIH Pub. No. 00–4754). Washington, DC: U.S. Department of Health and Human Services. Retrieved from **http://www.nationalreadingpanel.org/publications/subgroups.htm**

Pearson, P. D., & Johnson. (1978). *Teaching reading comprehension.* New York: Holt, Rinehart & Winston.

Reid, G. (2009). *Dyslexia: A practitioner's handbook, Fourth Edition.* New York: Jon Wiley & Sons.

Rose & Meyer. (2002). *Teaching every student in the digital age: Universal design for learning.* Alexandra, VA: ASCD.

Schoenbach, Greenleaf, Cziko, & Hurwitz. (1999). *Reading for understanding: A guide to improving reading in middle and high school classrooms.* San Francisco, CA: Jossey-Bass.

Sexton, Harris, & Graham. (1998). Self-regulated strategy development and the writing process: Effects on essay writing and attributions. *Exceptional Children, 64*(3).

Shaywitz, S. (2003). *Overcoming dyslexia.* New York: Vintage.

Snow, C., Burns, M., & Griffin, P. (Eds.). (1998). *Preventing reading difficulties in young children.* Washington, DC: National Academies.

Smith, D., Frey, N., Pumpian, I., & Fisher, D. (2017). *Building equity: Policies and practices to empower all learners.* Alexandria, VA: ASCD.